ROUTLEDGE LIBRARY EDITIONS:
SCOTLAND

I0124963

Volume 6

SCOTLAND BEFORE THE SCOTS

SCOTLAND BEFORE THE SCOTS
Being the Rhind Lectures for 1944

V. GORDON CHILDE

Routledge
Taylor & Francis Group
LONDON AND NEW YORK

First published in 1946 by Methuen

This edition first published in 2022
by Routledge
2 Park Square, Milton Park, Abingdon, Oxon OX14 4RN

and by Routledge
605 Third Avenue, New York, NY 10158

Routledge is an imprint of the Taylor & Francis Group, an informa business

© 1946 V. Gordon Childe

British Library Cataloguing in Publication Data
A catalogue record for this book is available from the British Library

ISBN: 978-1-03-206184-9 (Set)
ISBN: 978-1-00-321338-3 (Set) (ebk)
ISBN: 978-1-03-207028-5 (Volume 6) (hbk)
ISBN: 978-1-03-207034-6 (Volume 6) (pbk)
ISBN: 978-1-00-320504-3 (Volume 6) (ebk)

DOI: 10.4324/9781003205043

Publisher's Note
The publisher has gone to great lengths to ensure the quality of this reprint but points out that some imperfections in the original copies may be apparent.

Disclaimer
The publisher has made every effort to trace copyright holders and would welcome correspondence from those they have been unable to trace.

SCOTLAND BEFORE THE SCOTS

being
The Rhind Lectures for 1944

by

V. GORDON CHILDE

PROFESSOR OF PREHISTORIC ARCHAEOLOGY
UNIVERSITY OF EDINBURGH

METHUEN & CO. LTD. LONDON
36 Essex Street, Strand, W.C.2

First published in 1946

PRINTED IN GREAT BRITAIN BY
JARROLD AND SONS, LTD., NORWICH

PREFACE

THIS book embodies the substance of six Rhind Lectures delivered to the Society of Antiquaries of Scotland under the title, 'The Development of Tribal Society in Scotland in pre-Roman Times'. They were an attempt to present a slice of prehistory in a way quite novel to English readers. The prehistory of the British Isles was undoubtedly punctuated by a series of invasions. Accounts of it are liable to be so engrossed with tracing the successive invading groups to their Continental cradles and defining what contribution each introduced that they have little space left to relate what the several societies did when they got here. Our Soviet colleagues have criticized perhaps a little too harshly this idiosyncrasy of British prehistorians, but for their part have shown how the internal development of societies themselves can explain a wide range of archaeological facts. Their applications of Marxism to prehistory have produced narratives that seem more historical than a succession of invasions and are yet just as objective and solidly based on observed data. Accordingly when invited by the Society of Antiquaries to deliver the Rhind Lectures in Archaeology for 1944 on a subject relating to Scottish prehistory, I resolved to apply to it the method so successfully used by the late E. Krichevskiy, Kruglov, Podgayetskiy, Tretiakov, and other Marxists in Russian prehistory. Luckily the technical evidence has for the most part been already marshalled and digested so that its statement and analysis can be relegated to footnotes and appendices, leaving the text free for strictly historical action. The reader must judge whether the drama discharged be lively and convincing.

For the author it remains to acknowledge his indebtedness on the one hand to his Russian colleagues whose mastery both of archaeology and Marxism has been his inspiration and on the other to the Society of Antiquaries of Scotland not only for electing him Rhind Lecturer, but also for permitting him to illustrate this printed version of the course with reproductions of figures originally published in their *Proceedings* and other publications. Plates I, IV to XIII, and Figs. 2, 4, 5, 7, 8, 9, 11, 12, 13, 14, 16, 17, 18, 19, 20, 21, 22 and 24 are thus reproduced by permission of that Society which of course retains the copyright. The upper picture on Plate II is reproduced by permission of the Ministry of Works. My colleague, Mr. James Drummond, and Mr. Stuart Cruden have been kind enough to read the proofs.

EDINBURGH, *November 1945*

CONTENTS

CHAPTER I

CLASSIFICATION OF THE DATA

FOR reconstructing the life of forgotten, illiterate societies, archaeology offers the prehistorian an undigested mass of broken articles and ruined buildings—relics and monuments. Of this mass, bequeathed to us by the savage or barbarous past, part unfortunately still resists classification; no one knows, for instance, what the standing stones on the naked wine-dark moor were for, nor yet when they were set up. Here all objects of this sort, objects of speculation but not yet of knowledge, albeit regrettably numerous, will be simply ignored. All the rest are scientifically significant, but their value varies.

Some, representing means of production, dwellings, domestic furniture, and armament, are intrinsically interesting and germane to our purpose. Such will be duly described in the text. Others, on the contrary, are useful mainly as means of classifying the societies who made or used them. A full description of these might impede the narrative and weary a reader interested in history rather than technical archaeology. Most have already been illustrated, analysed, and discussed in my own *Prehistory of Scotland* or *Prehistoric Communities of the British Isles* and other works. Here I propose merely to name the more important with a few explanatory figures, relegating to appendices such technical discussion as is needed to correct and bring up to date older accounts, and to set forth the results of classification based upon them.

Since we hope to extort from the archaeological data a story of development, of a process in time, the most important basis of classification is the chronological. *Ex hypothesi*, being produced by illiterates, our relics and monuments bear no dates. Still, by application of appropriate techniques they can be arranged in a sequence—ultimately by an appeal to what is termed *stratigraphy*. For example, as at Skara Brae in Orkney, two or three houses may have been built one after another on the same spot so that their foundations lie one on top of another (Plate III, 2). The top house is obviously the latest and objects dropped and left upon its floor must be later in time than those dropped on the floor of the house below. Again, in a burial cairn—and the

I   I

archaeological record is largely derived from burials—we often find 'secondary graves' inserted in the body of the cairn or near its periphery; such graves and their contents are clearly later than the 'primary burial' under the very centre of the mound.

By such devices it is possible to distinguish six *stages* prior to the well-marked horizon of the Roman period. I use the word 'stages' advisedly. All over Scotland, indeed over most of the British Isles, the stages demonstrably follow one another in the same order; and they denote, as I hope to show, really consecutive phases in technical and economic progress. But we are not entitled to assume that they represent equal periods of time or were everywhere synchronous as measured against an absolute time-scale. On the contrary, serious discrepancies in the duration of each stage and substantial overlaps in time between the several natural regions must be admitted. All the contents, the culture, of each stage may be called *systadial* everywhere, but not synchronous. The Beaker culture in Orkney, for instance, is systadial with that in the Lothians but is probably several centuries later in time, perhaps indeed synchronous with the Urn culture that defines stage V south of the Forth.

Each of several stages is most easily defined and recognized by the burial rites, the forms of implements, and, best of all, the style of pottery vessels fashionable in it and it alone. These changing fashions or types thus serve as indicators wherever they turn up, telling the archaeologist to which stage everything associated with them should be assigned. The whole complex of graves or houses, tools, weapons, ornaments, found containing or with or in such leading types, is regarded as systadial and as belonging to the stage thus defined.

At the same time, within any given stage, more than one style of pottery, method of burial or type of axe may be fashionable but not at the same site nor in the same layer. Prehistorians can distinguish two or more assemblages of relics and monuments that have divergent distributions in space but belong to the same stage or period. Technically, such contemporary or systadial assemblages are termed *cultures*. Prehistorians assume that each culture represents a distinct people or society; the peculiarities of its domestic architecture, burial ritual, ceramic decoration or fashions of ornament reflect the divergencies of the traditions that constitute the spiritual unity of each group. Within stages I, II, and VI we shall certainly have to deal with several distinct societies; from stage III to V, however, the archaeological material is so uniform throughout Scotland that only one society need be recognized.

Stage I. The earliest peoples traceable in Scotland are very imperfectly represented by the scattered assemblages of implements termed mesolithic and microlithic. No monumental remains survive and the relics are mostly bits of flint and other durable material collected on sandy coasts or fields—doubtless only fragments of a richer and more varied equipment made largely of wood and other perishable materials. Despite the imperfections of the record, four groups can be distinguished— Larnians in Kintyre, 'Azilians' in Galloway, Ayrshire, and Argyll, Forest folk round the Forth and Tay estuaries and Tardenoisians widespread from Tweedside to Orkney. The high antiquity of the first three is guaranteed by geology; for they lived on the shore of the sea, when its waters stood some twenty-five feet higher than they do to-day. On the other hand, the Tardenoisians' microliths have analogies indeed in an equally ancient context in England and Belgium but they may have persisted here much later. Some indeed are in time not older than products of stages II and III, but even these were probably used by societies culturally pre-Neolithic, i.e. that had not achieved the economic and material advances characterizing stage II.

The succeeding stages are all confined to a later geological epoch when the distribution of land and sea at least was much the same as it is to-day. Stages II to V are best represented in graves. As it was the practice to bury with the departed his gear and food, the graves generally contain a representative selection of the tools, weapons, ornaments, and vessels fashionable at the time of burial. In their light, stray articles of the same types can be classified as systadial, and the list can be extended by the inclusion of other types found associated with the preceding in domestic sites or hoards.

Stage II. The funerary record begins with what are termed *chambered cairns*—very large piles of stones (or in Orkney earth), generally round or oval in plan, and sometimes 100 to 200 feet long (Plate IV, 1); all covered built stone chambers (Plate IV, 2) which served as *collective tombs*, family vaults used for successive interments probably over several generations. Not all the contents of these tombs are therefore contemporary or representative of stage II. In fact the latest interments in ten tombs (Nos. 37, 87, 106, 111, 253, 254, 255, 275, 286, 304) were accompanied by *Beakers*, an easily recognizable sort of vase that is more often found with contracted skeletons, buried individually in short cists, and that is here taken as distinctive of stage III. But the tombs themselves and the relics accompanying the first inter- ments in them are thereby shown to be older than stage III and therefore representative of stage II.

In plan and in the ritual practised within them the chambers covered by Scottish cairns agree generally with a famous series of sepulchral monuments widespread all over Atlantic Europe and round the North Sea. Many being built of very large un- dressed stones, the whole group is often called *megalithic*. That term is here applied to all the Scottish monuments, albeit some- times with little justification.

As the map (Fig. 1) shows, chambered cairns are virtually confined to the west and far northern coasts. Within this area my list records some 360 tombs divisible into two major groups on architectural as well as geographical grounds, 273 passage graves in the north and north-west, and 57 long cists in the south-west. Within the whole series, the undermentioned typo- logical and local subgroups can be distinguished: A, Heeled Cairns in Shetland (24); B1, Tripartite passage graves in Caith- ness and Orkney, of which thirteen are long-horned, the rest round or 'short-horned'; B2, Stalled Cairns in Eday, Rousay, and Westray; B3, the Unstan type on Rousay and Orkney Mainland (3); B4, the Quoyness type in Orkney (Mainland, Sanday, and Westray) (7 in all); C, 'Orthostatic' passage graves divisible into two local groups—C1, 68 in Sutherland and Easter Ross, includ- ing 18 long cairns; and C2, 39 in the Hebrides and Skye, of which 8 cairns are long; D, 'Tholoi' of the Clava type in the valleys of the Beauly, Ness, Nairn, and Spey (31); E, Segmented cists of the Clyde type generally covered by long cairns in Islay, Kintyre, Arran, and Bute, and on the northern shores of the Clyde and Loch Fyne (36); and F, Megalithic cists of the Solway type in Ayrshire and Galloway (see Appendix I).

Only 66 of these cairns have been excavated at all systemati- cally and only 35 have yielded any significant relics whatsoever. No relics of any kind nor even human remains are available from any tomb of the Clava or Solway type while the few relics from chambers of Quoyness type resist classification. The status of these three groups is therefore uncertain. In representative tombs of all the remaining groups, excavation has disclosed human skeletons and furniture that may safely be regarded as primary. This includes stone axes (5 tombs), leaf-shaped flint arrow-heads

FIG. 1. DISTRIBUTION OF CHAMBERED CAIRNS IN SCOTLAND

CHAMBERED CAIRNS
■ Northern Types
▦ Northern Types, Long
◆ Quoyness Type
● Clava Type
▲ Clyde Type
▼ Solway Type

PENTLAND FIRTH

NORTH EAST SCOTLAND

GREAT GLEN

R. TAY

STRATHMORE

R. CLYDE

LOTHIANS

(10 tombs), plain, round-bottomed vases of leathery 'Atlantic' or 'Western' pottery (24 tombs), closely allied to the early Neolithic pottery of England that is called Windmill Hill ware. With the latter, and equally primary, go sometimes decorated vases of two kinds: *Beacharra* ware (Plate I, 2) mainly in the Clyde group but also in the Hebrides and perhaps represented by one sherd from tomb No. 53 in Orkney and *Unstan* ware (Plate I, 3), principally in Orkney and Caithness but found also on a domestic site in North Uist.

Some tombs, however, contain also not only Beaker pottery that defines stage III, but also other types that on English analogies should be later than stage II: stone mace-heads pierced with a cylindrical hole for the shaft (Nos. 39, 106, 112, 303) (4); plano-convex flint knives (Nos. 33, 300, 304, 312); flint knives with polished edges (Nos. 63, 112, 115, 303), and flint arrow-heads derived from a mesolithic chisel-ended form (Nos. 112, 115). These relics must further illustrate the use of the tombs for burial after the close of stage II. But the leathery pottery and the decorated wares (and with reserve leaf-shaped flint arrow-heads) may be regarded as defining stage II as much as the tombs themselves.

Such typical western pottery has been found indeed outside tombs in domestic contexts at Townhead, Rothesay (Bute), Eilean an Tighe (North Uist), Wideford Hill (Orkney), and in Strathspey,[1] all within the megalithic province. But it occurs beyond it in one or other of our megalithic provinces: at Hedderwick (Dunbar), Bantaskine (Falkirk), East Finnercy, Dunnecht, Easterton of Roseisle (Moray), and Culbin Sands. These latter discoveries and a very few isolated long cairns are the only direct indications of the existence of societies in stage II of western type outside the area defined by the concentration of chambered cairns. A relative abundance of leaf-shaped arrow-heads in north-eastern Scotland cannot be taken as proof of the presence of such societies since both in Scotland and England leaf-shaped arrow-heads have been found in Cinerary Urns, distinctive of stage V.

On the other hand, other Neolithic societies are now known that may have taken the place of megalith-builders in eastern Scotland. In Orkney, the remarkable culture first recognized at Skara Brae has now been found flourishing at Rinyo on Rousay[2] below a level (Plate III, 2), on which stood the first Beaker to

---

[1] *Proc. Soc. Ant. Scot.*, lxxi, 367.   [2] ibid., lxxiii, 26.

define stage III in Orkney. It therefore belongs to stage II. Now, pottery of the type distinctive of Skara Brae has turned up also in East Lothian and abundantly in south-eastern England. There must then have been villages like Skara Brae between the Forth and the Pentland Firth, but, being built of perishable wood and not of stone as in the treeless northern isles, they will be hard to find. Their inhabitants perhaps have dropped the curious carved stone balls found astray in such numbers in north-east Scotland and Strathmore, as similar balls have been found at Skara Brae.

Another style of pottery, Peterborough ware, is known to be pre-Beaker in England and there defines a distinct Neolithic culture. Sherds of this fabric have been collected from Hedder-wick, Glenluce Sands (Wigtonshire), and Shewelton Moor (Ayrshire), but the circumstances of their discovery do not allow us to demonstrate their attribution to stage II in Scotland nor to define further the culture they should represent.

Stage III is defined archaeologically by the Beaker pottery (Plate V) that is found with the latest interments in a few chambered cairns and on the latest floor of a Neolithic house at Rinyo. Beakers most usually accompany single skeletons, buried in short cists (Plate VI, 2), sometimes in flat graves, sometimes covered by round cairns, occasionally intruded into the cairns covering Megalithic chambers. The persons buried with them belong to a new physical type, a new race in fact, round-headed in contrast to the long-headed folk who were the first to be buried in chambered cairns.

Beakers, more or less like ours, are found generally with round-headed skeletons all over Great Britain and in Sicily, Upper Italy, Sardinia, the Iberian Peninsula, south France, Brittany, Holland, north Germany, Jutland, and Central Europe, but are rare in Ireland. They vary considerably in form and decoration. These variations can be used not only to define local groups or cultures, discussed in Appendix II, but also to distinguish chronological phases; Beakers that diverge conspicuously from the general British standard or are more than usually clumsy in shape or negligent in decoration are considered to be late or degenerate though no direct stratigraphical proof is available in Scotland.

In England, Beaker graves often contain other distinctive gear: bowmen's wrist-guards (Plate V, 2), tanged-and-barbed arrow-heads, flint daggers, and bronze knife-daggers. While these are found in Scotland, too, they cannot be used to extend the list of burials attributable to stage III. No flint dagger has been found in any Scottish grave; the arrow-heads were used also in stages IV and V. Bronze daggers occur with Food Vessels, too, and, being associated here only with 'late' Beakers, should probably be assigned to stage IV (see Appendix VI). Other relics associated with Beakers occur also with Food Vessels—indeed more commonly.

This means that some Beakers are contemporary with some Food Vessels so that there is an overlap in time between stages III and IV. Indeed, if Beaker burials in general illustrate stage III, some must be so late as to be assigned more properly to IV. Table II shows a fantastic disproportion between Beakers and Food Vessels in north-east Scotland. It must mean that many Aberdeenshire Beakers are contemporary with Food Vessels elsewhere. Here, indeed, the Beaker culture must have maintained its purity so much longer than anywhere else, that some Beaker graves must be considered as systadial, as well as synchronous, with Food Vessel graves of stage IV elsewhere.

Apart from round cairns and short cists, Beakers also occur on domestic sites and within some of the curious 'Recumbent Stone Circles' of north-east Scotland (see Appendix III). These consist of complex and very irregular rings of upright stones always combined with a very large block lying horizontal between the two largest uprights (Plate VI, 1). They were undoubtedly used for burials after cremation, but it is not quite certain whether this was their original function nor, if it were, whether the Beakers actually accompanied the primary interments. Even if they did, the monuments may well belong to stage IV since, as we have just seen, Beakers were still current in the region then and cremation is more proper to IV than III.

Stage IV is marked by the replacement of Beakers by Food Vessels in short cists that may now contain cremated remains. These vases are much less homogeneous in form and decoration than are Beakers, but no convincing scheme of chronological classification can be established. Among 220 well-preserved Scottish Food Vessels, three groups can be recognized with some confidence. At least 105 *Vases* closely resemble in form and decoration the commonest Food Vessels from north-eastern England; these constitute 'type B'. On the other hand, I can cite 20 Bowl-shaped Vessels 'type A' (Plate VII, 1), to which there are more analogies in Ireland than in England. Thirdly, some 38 vessels seem to stand out as a predominantly Scottish type, intermediate between A and B, which may be designated type C (Plate VII, 2). The rest are so amorphous that they are conveniently described as 'Beaker-Food Vessel hybrids' (Bfh) (Appendix IV). A single Scottish specimen of the peculiarly Irish type, termed E by Abercromby, being found in a typical urnfield of stage V, must be attributed to that stage.

Various circumstances allow us to extend the inventory of stage IV beyond graves actually containing Food Vessels and their contents. Crescentic 'jet' necklaces (Plate VIII, 1), accompanied Food Vessels in nine or ten graves, and have only once been found with any other sort of funerary pottery—a B Beaker (No. 194). The remaining graves containing such necklaces may therefore be assigned to stage IV. Then Food Vessel graves often occur in groups of three or four; sometimes, indeed, one cist will contain a Food Vessel and the next a jet necklace but no pottery (65). Again, several burials in virgin soil, including one or more Food Vessels, may be covered by the same cairn (86-9, 79-80, 204-9). In a few such cemeteries, indeed, some burials may be contained in Urns proper to stage V (14, 150, 170, 238). But, in general, where the unfurnished graves are full-sized cists, all interments in such cemeteries may be attributed to the Food Vessel culture. Both extensions have been included in my list of 322 graves of stage IV.

Further extensions are possible. As basket-shaped metal ear-rings were associated with Food Vessels in Northumberland,[1] we may assign to the same context not only a famous burial at Orton, Moray, but also a hoard of bronzes, including such earrings, found at Migdale, in Sutherland.[2] Hence the types of bronze weapons and ornaments found in this hoard must have been current in stage IV, and the same applies to the contents of the hoard of Auchnacree, Angus,[3] which is typologically contemporary with Migdale. Bronze knife-daggers, like those from Achnacree, are also associated with Food Vessels in at least one grave, but only with very late and degenerate Beakers. Hence the other burials containing such daggers probably fall within stage IV (Appendix VI, A).

As crescentic jet necklaces belong to the Food Vessel complex, so must the handsome gold collars or lunulae (Plate VIII, 2), since Craw and Clark have demonstrated that these are just translations of necklaces or vice versa. So all the leading metal tools, weapons, and ornaments, classed by Callander as 'Bronze Age II',

[1] Childe, *P.C.B.I.*, 125.   [2] *Proc.*, xxxv, 266.   [3] *Proc.*, lvi, 351.

were in use during our stage IV. Among these Callander includes halberds, certainly imported from Ireland. Though these are not associated with other distinctive types of metal ware nor with funerary pottery in the British Isles, their attribution to stage IV can be justified in a roundabout way (Appendix VII).

A quite different and hitherto unrecognized group of burials can now be classified as belonging to stage IV. These consist of long—but not Megalithic—cists designed to contain a skeleton extended at full length, not doubled up as in short cists. At least one such grave was furnished with a halberd while the ritual is parallel to that observed in a group of contemporary graves in England (see Appendix V). Two other very rich burials contained daggers similar to some found with extended skeletons and more developed than the normal knife-dagger of stage IV, but still typologically earlier than anything appropriate to stage V.

Cremated interments contained in specially shaped *Cinerary Urns* (Plate XI) have been found on the edge, or high up in the body, of cairns (Urns, Nos. 300, 311, 503, 618, 516), originally heaped over burials accompanied by Beakers (101a, 246) or Food Vessels (Nos. 165, 224, 284),[1] or, in one case, by daggers appropriate to the extended burials just mentioned. These cases provide the stratigraphical proof that such Cinerary Urns are later than stage IV. They are accordingly taken as distinctive of stage V. Most of these urns, however, come from flat graves and a large number from cemeteries of such termed *urnfields* (Plate X, 1).

My list of 664 graves of stage V (Appendix VIII) includes in addition to cremations in Cinerary Urns such unurned cremations as have been recorded in urnfields. Owing to the haphazard manner in which most of these cemeteries have been examined, the number of such included is small, but in reality at the well-excavated urnfield of Loanhead, no less than 19 out of 31 cremations (77–107) had been deposited in the bare earth. Many of the urns are known only from old reports that by specifying the size of the vessels or their inverted position leave no doubt that they were in fact Cinerary Urns, but naturally do not suffice to define the precise variety; others are too fragmentary to classify. Of the remainder, the immense majority belong to the Overhanging Rim family that is supposed to have started in southwestern England. The degeneration of these urns has been traced through some five typological stages. The oldest of these is

[1] cf. also R. C. Fife, 497, and N.S.A., ix, 268.

unrepresented in Scotland, but stage II, with well-defined shoulder and concave neck (Plate XI, 1), is found as far north as Aberdeenshire, though collared and biconical urns (Fig. 14), belonging to stages IV and V, unrepresented in southern England, are rather commoner in Scotland than earlier forms. The late forms are alone represented north of the Beauly Firth and exceed the early forms in the proportion of 8 to 5 in north-east Scotland and of 8 to 3 in Ayrshire. In Fife and the Lothians, the proportions are reversed to 15 to 8 and 4 to 3 respectively. This seems to prove that the urn fashion, and perhaps the people who followed it, did spread gradually northward and further emphasizes the lateness in time of many Scottish graves of stage V.

The curious ritual vessels, termed Pigmy Vessels (Plate X, 2), often found in urns of the Overhanging Rim family or in cemeteries of such, may also be regarded as, on the whole, English in idea. Some in Scotland, however, are nothing but very small Food Vessels and will be termed Diminished Food Vessels (77, 133, 164, 309).

But at least 25 urns, including 9 from north-east Scotland, are Enlarged Food Vessels (Fig. 14, 1 and 4), which occur also in northern England. Finally, 13 urns from Scotland belong to what Abercromby terms the Encrusted type (Plate XI, 2). Such derive their form from the Enlarged Food Vessel, but the technique and the motives of their decoration have been taken over from the 'Neolithic' tradition of Skara Brae. Half come from north of the Tay, where we saw other reasons to assume a strong Skara Brae element. The emergence or re-emergence of this tradition in stage V shows how long it must have persisted or how late a culture, belonging stadially to II, may be in absolute time.

Conversely, Cinerary Urns being disproportionately rare in the West Highlands and the Clyde Firth province (Table II), we must admit that many Food Vessels there must be contemporary with Urns in other provinces. Presumably the Food Vessel culture and the social structures appropriate to stage IV persisted there throughout most of the time occupied by stage V, perhaps indeed till the establishment of the Iron Age cultures distinctive of stage VI, which seem no later in Morvern and Bute than round the Tay estuary.

The deposition of funerary gifts seems to have gone out of fashion in Scotland by stage V as in the rest of Europe during the Late Bronze Age; in less than fifty graves did any weapon or ornament accompany interments in Cinerary Urns. Among the rare grave goods are flint arrow-heads, generally barbed and tanged and with serrated edges but with urn 361 also leaf-shaped (Plate XIII, 1); stone mace-heads or battle-axes; leaf-shaped bronze razors (3, 29, 131, 275, 276, 328, 410, 464); bone toggles transversely perforated or looped (23, 72, 85, 148, 191, 136), and star-shaped or segmented beads of vitreous material, not identical with the imported beads of Mediterranean fayence found in England.

On the other hand, numerous swords, socketed axes, shields, cauldrons, and other metal products of Late Bronze Age type have been found stray or in hoards (Plate XII, 1). The relation of these to the funerary record cannot be established directly. But the typological development of metal tools and weapons taken in conjunction with foreign analogies and the absolute chronology discussed below justifies indirectly the attribution of this metal ware to stage V. This stage, in fact, represents the end of the archaeologist's Bronze Age. With stage VI we reach the Iron Age and therewith the character of the record changes.

One burial in the urnfield at Loanhead of Daviot and several in the adjacent Stone Circle were contained in flat-rimmed, unornamented, barrel-shaped urns better fired than the average Overhanging Rim Urn and set mouth upwards. In the Largs urnfield, too, seven urns, buried together mouth up in an oval boulder-lined pit, were of similar form and fabric as is an ossuary from Duff House, Banffs. As pottery of the same kind was recovered from an Iron Age bloomery at Loanhead, these burials must be assigned to stage VI, even though cognate wares were associated with ornaments of final Bronze Age character in the Sculptor's Cave, Covesea (Moray). With these cremations the funerary record breaks off altogether, and our picture of stage VI has to be constructed entirely from domestic sites. We just do not know where and how the inhabitants of these were buried nor how long after their first occupation the old Bronze Age societies may have gone on burying their dead in urnfields.

In the occupational record we dispose of a vast number of conspicuous monuments, most notably defensive works. Only a tiny fraction of these have been at all scientifically or profitably excavated. In most cases the nature of the site—an exposed and rocky hill-top—is highly unfavourable to the conservation of relics; these are liable to be washed away while erosion also destroys the ancient surface soil in which the foundations of timber buildings could otherwise have been detected. Our acid soils are destructive of objects of bone and of iron. By the nature of the case only broken and discarded fragments would have been left lying about for us to find. In a relatively large area it is very much a matter of chance if a trial excavation on a modest scale uncover a patch where habitation refuse has been preserved.

Then most sites have been occupied continuously or with intermissions over many generations. In the thin soil a stratigraphical sequence of layers can seldom accumulate, and any such that may exist is liable to have been disturbed by digging drains or later foundations. Only very meticulous planning can enable the excavator, in the most favourable circumstances, to disentangle the architectural phases of successive recon- structions. Accordingly, excava- tions in such monuments yield, as a rule, only an undifferen- tiated mass of objects that can be classified chronologically only by comparison with those from England and the neigh- bouring Continental regions,

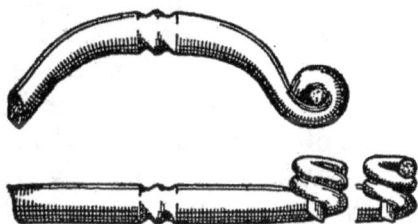

FIG. 2.
LA TÈNE I BROOCH, RAHOY. ¼

where reliable chronological sequences have been established. Since the foundation date of a monument is given by the earliest relic found within it, we can treat as pre-Roman and so repre- sentative of stage VI all sites that have yielded relics thus classifi- able as La Tène. The very exiguous list of such sites—one crannog, three hill-top forts, four Gallic forts—can luckily be enlarged by the inclusion of whole classes of monuments that can, as a rule, be recognized without excavation.

The most conspicuous group is constituted by the sixty Gallic and vitrified forts. Eight have been excavated with some success; three (34, 46, 48) yielded La Tène I brooches (Fig. 2), a type that went out of fashion on the Continent about 250 B.C.; ring head pins come from three (24, 46, 48), and an iron imitation of a socketed bronze axe from one (34); on the other hand, objects characteristic of the Roman period were conspicuously absent from all save two (24, 38), in both of which there is superficial evidence for the insertion of secondary constructions.

A 'Gallic wall' is here understood as a rampart consisting of two parallel masonry faces laced together by transverse beams, the interspace being filled up with rubble and timber (Plate XIV, 1). Probably all Scottish forts, here classed as Gallic, were defended with such a rampart. An improvement, probably developed in Gaul after 100 B.C., in which the transverse and internal beams are bolted together, is represented in Scotland only at Burghead. A second variety in which the masonry is supported by a frame of uprights as well as transverse tie beams has been revealed at the Camps, Edgerston (Roxb.), but is not certainly as old as the type described above.

Ten years ago I suggested that Gallic and vitrified forts represented the same culture. Now Dr. Bersu's Continental researches and W. Thorneycroft's experiments have shown that what is called a vitrified rampart is just a Gallic wall that has been burned. If the timber in such a wall be ignited in a wind, such as normally rages over Scottish hill-tops, the interior becomes a veritable furnace and generates such heat that the stones of the core melt and fuse together into solid masses. It is just such masses of fused stones that define 'vitrified forts'.

As vitrification can easily be recognized by mere inspection and has been persistently sought for during two centuries, the recorded examples afford a welcome extension of the list of sites representative of stage VI. But only if the wall be ignited and only if it be built of fusible stone, will vitrification occur at all, and its extent will depend on the wind blowing at the time of the conflagration, for a sort of blast is needed to generate the requisite heat. If the core be not consolidated by fusion and the nature of the structure revealed by vitrified stones, the remains of a Gallic wall are hard to recognize. For such walls will collapse when the tie-beams decay, even if not burned, and only exceptionally, as in Abernethy and Monifieth, will the faces remain standing to a sufficient height to show the sockets for the tie-beams; and these could, as a rule, only be exposed by the removal of masses of stone fallen from the upper courses. Since vitrification depends upon a conjuncture of geological, meteorological, and historical conditions, many unvitrified Gallic forts may await discovery. An uncertain number of hill-forts, especially such as are defended by rectilinear ramparts such as are so characteristic of a number of vitrified forts, may really belong to this group.

Furthermore, many hill-tops, originally defended by Gallic walls, have been occupied or reoccupied in Roman times, the Dark Ages, or still later. Castle Urquhart occupies the site of a vitrified fort. On the Laws of Monifieth, a small ring fort amongst the stones in which vitrified masses were observed,[1] had been

[1] *Proc.*, iii, 446.

erected within the partially vitrified enceinte, probably in post-Roman times. Similarly, at Dun Skeig, lumps of vitrified matter taken from the adjacent Gallic fort can be seen in the rubble core of the well-preserved ring-fort on the same hill-top. At Dun Macuisneachean, the small oval enclosure measuring only 135 by 90 feet, that Smith[1] calls 'the central living space', seems to be a similar intrusion in larger and earlier work since he writes that its 'east wall had been rebuilt [sic] partly at least by using some of the waste of the vitrified part'. The Royal Commission[2] has recently reported similar secondary works at Auldhill, Portencross, and Kildoun. The objects of Romano-Caledonian or later character from Dun Macuisneachean and Monifieth can naturally be attributed to the secondary occupations thus architecturally attested.

Nevertheless it would be premature to infer that the ingenious method of construction had been forgotten or abandoned in A.D. 80, and hence that every vitrified fort is necessarily anterior to that date.

Relics of pre-Roman type have also been recovered from two large hill-top forts—Traprain and Bonchester Hill—while a third, Burnswark, must be accepted as pre-Roman since the legions under Agricola seem to have besieged it. Unfortunately, the nature of the pre-Roman ramparts has not been defined at any of these sites while the criteria of size and location are rather too vague for the identification of other sites as pre-Roman. More-over, the relics recovered from them do not add much to our picture of stage VI. Though the excavations at Traprain pro-duced many relics, most were of the Roman period. The strati-graphy observed served generally only to subdivide the latter; at one point alone was the pre-Roman period distinguished stratigraphically.

Some crannogs or lake-dwellings must, on the strength of Irish analogies, have been inhabited during stage VI, if not earlier, but the Scottish evidence for such occupation is too slender to afford any reliable additions to our picture of pre-Roman Scotland. On the other hand, those conspicuous and still im-pressive monuments, the brochs or Pictish towers, were for the most part built before the Roman invasion under Agricola. Two lines of evidence, developed in Appendix IX, converge to prove that the broch culture had been established in the extreme north of Scotland, and already spread to the Lowlands before A.D. 80.

[1] *Proc.*, xi, 300; cf. plan, in vol. xii, pl. I.   [2] ibid., lxxvii, 39.

It not only enlarges our list of monuments and relics illustrative of stage VI, but also brings the Northern Isles once more within the frame of our stadial classification. On the other hand, since brochs are not the earliest monuments from which iron objects have been recovered, at least in Shetland, the broch culture may be regarded as representative of a distinct subdivision of stage VI, say VIb.

THE CULTURE SEQUENCE IN ORKNEY AND SHETLAND

The sequence of stages based on the funerary record needs adjustment when applied to Orkney, Shetland, and the Hebrides, since there Food Vessels and Cinerary Urns, taken as distinctive of stages IV and V, do not occur in the Mainland form and the metal weapons and ornaments that formed such a valuable supplement to the ceramic evidence are never found in insular graves. But in Orkney and Shetland there are cist-graves and tumuli. Some, admittedly, belong to the pagan Vikings and fall outside the scope of this survey. But others must represent the sequel to the chambered cairns of stage II and therefore correspond to our stages III–V. Among these, four groups may be distinguished.

Group A consists of short cists of normal size, over 2′ 6″ long. Such contain skeletons and generally nothing else, but a fragment of a Beaker was found in one at Scatness, Shetland.[1] They may therefore be partially, at least, systadial with graves of stage III on the Scottish mainland. Some full-sized cists contain cremated bones as well as, or instead of, skeletons, and constitute group B. Some contain small bowl-shaped vessels of steatite (a soft stone occurring in nature in Shetland), which seem to fulfil the function of Food Vessels (Plate VII, 4). They may therefore be held to represent stage IV. To group C, I would assign smaller cists, 15 to 21 inches square (Plate VI, 3), containing cremated bones, sometimes enclosed in clay or steatite urns (Plate XI, 3). Finally, cremation burials in simple pits, inurned or not, might be classed as group D. They should be systadial with our urnfields of stage V, the larger steatite or clay urns being comparable to Cinerary Urns while some smaller steatite vessels in group C might be regarded as 'Pigmy Vessels' (cf. Appendix X).

If these comparisons be accepted, our picture of life in stages IV and V can be enriched by material gathered from habitation sites such as on the mainland are painfully rare. For the northern

[1] *Proc.*, lxvii, 34.

sepulchral sequence can, very tentatively, be correlated with a domestic record disclosed by Dr. Curle's excavations at Jarlshof, the southern tip of Shetland. There he laid bare six dwellings. Each had been occupied for some time and had undergone several reconstructions so that the chronological relations between the several dwellings are hard to decipher. Two house-types are represented—an earlier, courtyard house, Nos. I, IIIa, and V (Fig. 11), and a later, roughly circular form approximating to the later wheel-house associated in Nos. IIIb–c and VI with souterrains.

There are also three technological phases: in (i) no bronze was used at the site but a great variety of well-made tools of slate, quartz, and other stones. In (ii) a bronze-smith set up his workshop in the village and manufactured on the spot swords, socketed axes, and knives of Late Bronze Age forms, scattering about fragments of the clay moulds used in making them. Finally (iii) slag proves the practice of iron smelting too, though at first bronze implements were still being cast. Phase (i) alone is represented by courtyard house V, where no mould fragments were found and by the earliest occupation of I. While dwelling I was still standing, the smith arrived and converted it into his workshop. During the period of bronze working this dwelling was reconstructed for a second time and another courtyard house, No. III, was erected. Many mould fragments were found on its first floor (IIIa), but in one annexe[1] some iron slag turned up too. Dwelling III was subsequently remodelled on a more circular plan and a souterrain dug under its floor after bronze working had apparently ceased, while dwelling VI, too, yielded evidence of iron smelting but not of bronze casting.

Now subrectangular steatite bowls of the same shape as one from a grave of group B at Little Asta, Shetland[2] (Plate VII, 4), were found in dwelling V. So if the foregoing equations be accepted, the earlier courtyard houses and the 'pre-metallic' industrial phase at Jarlshof should be systadial with the Food Vessel culture and stage IV on the mainland. The bronze types, manufactured in the succeeding industrial phase, would in turn be appropriate to stage V. Finally, since all the dwellings seem older than the erection of the broch of Jarlshof that would belong to the last half of stage VI, the period of iron smelting and dwellings IIIb–c and VI could be treated as systadial with the earlier part of stage VI.

[1] *Proc.*, lxviii, 303.   [2] *Proc.*, lxvi, 72.

Calder's recent excavations on the Calf of Eday allow these results to be applied to Orkney too. Stevenson[1] points out that some of the pottery from the so-called 'Potter's Workshop' there is strictly parallel to that from dwelling IIIb of the early iron-working phase at Jarlshof, while other sherds from this site might 'have come from the Neolithic site of Rinyo'. The structure from which the sherds come is akin to Jarlshof dwellings III, IV, and VI, but even more explicitly a wheel-house, being in fact divided into nine compartments by radial walls (Fig. 11). It shows not only that houses of this plan were being erected in Orkney in stage VIa but also that the other wheel-houses found in Orkney, and more frequently in the Hebrides, represent a native type in the isles, typologically anterior to the brochs whatever the stadial and chronological position of individual dwellings (most would seem to be later than A.D. 80). Accordingly, the insular and mainland records can be compared in the following table:

I

Mainland Stage	Insular Graves	Domestic Record
II	Chambered Cairns (Stalled and Unstan types)	Skara Brae and Rinyo
III	? Chambered cairns of Quoyness type Cists with skeletons	
IV	Cists with cremations or inhumations and small steatite bowls	Jarlshof. Dwellings V and Ia
V	Small cists or pits with cremation in clay or steatite urns	Ib-c and IIIa

ABSOLUTE CHRONOLOGY

The classification into stages exhibits the succession of events. Can we give dates for these events and estimate the durations of the stages? Any answers to these questions are provisional and at best approximate. They depend, in the long run, on the historical records of Egypt, Mesopotamia, Greece, and Rome. By devious ways, objects fashionable among our illiterate ancestors can be connected with those current in the eastern Mediterranean at known historical periods, but only indirectly and through many equally barbarian intermediaries on the continent of Europe.

[1] *Proc.*, lxxiii, 182.

Some of the highly technical arguments will be sketched in Appendix IX. The tentative conclusions are as follows.

Stage VI ends, ex hypothesi, with an historical event, the arrival of the Roman legions under Agricola in A.D. 80. The beginning of the stage is limited by the fashions, especially in brooches, introduced by the builders of Gallic forts. On the Continent such brooches were scarcely current before 300 B.C. and were abandoned soon after 250, but in a provincial area they might easily have survived till 100. Hence stage VI began not before 300 and not necessarily before 100 B.C. Part of an imported bronze cup, of a type current on the Continent in the earlier Hallstatt period, was found in the hoard of Adabrock, Lewis, with tools and weapons here assigned to stage V (Plate XII, 1). Accordingly, stage V should have begun before 600 B.C. if that be the date of the transition from early to late Hallstatt abroad. Finally, if stage IV be partly contemporary with the Wessex culture of southern England, its beginnings must go back to at least 1400 B.C., since the Wessex culture can be approximately dated through commercial contacts with the east Mediterranean. Any earlier dates are only guesses, save that an antiquity of the order of eight to seven thousand years can be assigned on geological grounds to the Larnians of Kintyre, who raised the curtain on stage I.

GEOGRAPHICAL CLASSIFICATION

The societies we are about to consider not only developed in time but were also distributed in space. The main natural features governing their distribution—the sinuosities of the coast-line and mountain chains—are conspicuous enough on a bathyorographical map and can be followed with the aid of the 100- and 200-metre contour lines included in the distribution maps in this volume. But the reader should recall that great tracts of swamp and dense forest, no longer existing, once constituted even more formidable barriers than firths or ranges. Then, beside the familiar division into Highlands and Lowlands, charmingly indicated on eighteenth-century maps by the 'whisky line', a contrast between east and west is no less significant.

Fronting the North Sea on the east are relatively low-lying areas separated from one another by hills or firths. It will be convenient to recognize the following: The Tweed basin constitutes one such unit, much encumbered by damp woodland and lying partly south of the Border. Beyond the Lammermuirs and

Moorfoots begins another province, the Lothians, and across the Forth a third—Fife with Kinross and Clackmannan—extending to the Firth of Tay. From that firth the coastal plain and, beyond the discontinuous ridge of the Sidlaws, Strathmore form another province extending inland to the Grampians and northward to the Mounth. Crossing that range we enter a self-contained bit of Lowlands—north-east Scotland—with a marked individuality of its own. West of the Spey, Moray and the southern shores of the Beauly Firth offer a smaller lowland province, while north-west of that firth the Black Isle and Easter Ross and Sutherland constitute another restricted lowland area. Finally, north-east of Morven and the Ord lies the plain of Caithness, extending across the Pentland Firth to Orkney.

Sharply contrasted herewith are the West Highlands, where the only cultivable tracts are narrow glens and strips of raised beach hemmed in and mutually isolated by rugged cliffs, forests, and swamps. A similar structure is encountered in Galloway and north-western Ayrshire. But the Clyde valley returns rather to the Lowland pattern. So would the central Ayrshire plain, lower Nithsdale, and lower Annandale, but that in early times these were cumbered by damp oakwoods of excessive size and density.

On the west, accordingly, intercourse between the isolated units of settlement has always been far easier by sea than by land. For the sea unites as much as it divides, once man has learnt to fashion any sort of boat. In particular the comparatively shel-tered Firth of Clyde, with its arms Loch Fyne and Loch Long, unites into a single province Kintyre, Arran, Bute, Cumbrae, Cowal. And, in a real sense, this unity extends across the narrow and not always stormy channel to Antrim.

Obviously, the several provinces of the North Sea frontage too, in so far as they were connected in prehistoric times, were linked across the Firths of Forth, Tay, and Moray, rather than round them. You can see Orkney from the Banffshire coast. Roads round the Beauly, Cromarty, and Dornoch Firths are recent innovations; the old route crossed by ferries at Fort George, Cromarty, and Dornoch. Both coasts of the Moray Firth belonged to a single cultural province in stage II, judged by sepulchral architecture.

II
DISTRIBUTION OF BRONZE AGE GRAVES

Province	Graves of Stage		
	III	IV	V
North of Beauly Firth . .	14	17	29
Moray	14	15	10
North-east Scotland . .	91	18	97
Tay to Mounth . . .	19	51	34
Fife, Kinross, etc. . . .	9	29	176
Lothians	20	40	98
Tweed Basin . . .	17	30	31 (incomplete)
West Highlands (including Skye, but not the Outer Isles) .	7	20	3
Clyde Firth province . .	9	41	9
Clyde Valley	6	32	57
Ayrshire	5	11	76
Galloway (with Dumfries-shire)	5	15	37
Upper Tay and Upper Forth basins	5	10	6
Totals	221	329	663

CHAPTER II

STONE AGE SOCIETIES

DURING the Ice Age Scotland, covered with glaciers, had been simply uninhabitable. The earliest societies we can expect to find, and do in fact find, here must be immigrants who arrived after the glaciers had receded. As by that time a wide North Sea already separated Britain from Scandinavia and the Low Countries, the most likely routes for immigrants would be land-ways from England or across the North Channel from Ireland. And they would naturally arrive with cultures, material and social, already developed. These early colonists have left very small impression on the archaeological record—little in fact but very small flints. How they lived we can, in general, only infer; hypotheses as to their social organization would have to be based on still more indirect evidence.

The earliest definable groups indeed seem confined to the shores of the enlarged post-glacial sea. That may, of course, seem so only because the high strands from which the sea has since receded offer convenient collecting grounds for relics. It may, on the other hand, indicate a dependence on fishing and the collection of crabs and shell-fish and at the same time a preference for foreshores that wind and spray had bared of embarrassing forest growth; for axes, adzes, or other tools, for dealing with timber are conspicuously absent from the remains left by most groups.

Several distinct groups, not all synchronous, have to be distinguished chiefly by divergencies in the traditional equipment with which they tried to adapt themselves to similar environments. The first arrivals, the Larnians in Kintyre, not only shared industrial traditions with the Mesolithic population of northern Ireland, but also used Antrim[1] flint. Hence they were presumably advanced enough in technology to be able to cross and recross the stormy North Channel and economically to obtain supplies of this essential raw material from overseas, perhaps by barter with kindred tribes or clans. Once obtained, the flint was worked locally in Kintyre. In any case the contacts between the Clyde coasts and Ireland that become so significant in stages II, IV,

[1] *Proc.*, lxxv, 61.

and V, reach back to the very beginnings of Scottish prehistory. Flint, obtained with such peril, must have been very precious. The Kintyre Larnians accordingly displayed their ingenuity in finding and using as substitutes quartz and other refractory stones of which local supplies were available. Moreover a few *microburins* suggest to Lacaille[1] that these predominantly Irish colonists were already mingled with, or at least in contact with, Tardenoiseans from England, since the *microburin* is foreign to the pure Larnian tradition of flint work.

The so-called Azilians or Obanians are slightly better known. We have found at least the shallow caves in which they sheltered round Oban and holes for stakes that may have supported some wind-break or tent of brushwood or skins on the exposed beach of Oransay. The food refuse from their encampments indicates an economy based on collecting shell-fish, hunting seals, deer, badgers, boars, otters, wild cats, fowling, and fishing. In the chase, they were helped, like other systadial groups from Portugal to the Crimea, by dogs. One fishing implement was a spear or harpoon of bone or rarely stag's antler (Plate I, 1). Dug-out canoes, rafts, or skin boats, were certainly available. Flint could be got in Mull and Morvern.

Judged by their fishing tackle these colonists should have come from France and have Atlantic kinsmen. Yet, here again, there are hints of a mixture of traditions; the common substitution of bone for antler as the material for 'harpoons', the form of one from Oransay (Plate I, 1), and an antler axe from Risga,[2] are all more proper to the North European plain and the Baltic-North Sea coasts than to the Atlantic, and may at least have been copied from the equipment of immigrants from that side established on our eastern coast. After all, only a very narrow isthmus separated the Forth Estuary from the Clyde and Lomond Firths. And whalers from the east had made their way five miles west of Stirling, dropping an antler-axe beside the carcase of a stranded whale. But otherwise we know even less about these immigrants than about the Obanians.

Of the Tardenoiseans still less is known though their relics are the most widespread. Microliths have been collected from the Tweed and Galloway to Caithness and Orkney,[3] but not even bones or shells are associated with them. Only from foreign

---

[1] *Proc.*, lxxv, 72.
[2] Information from A. D. Lacaille; in Hunterian Museum, Glasgow.
[3] *Proc.*, lxxviii, 5.

analogies can we deduce that their makers were hunters and collectors and that some microliths served to arm arrows.

So several distinct societies are disclosed in the archaeological record for stage I, but all apparently food-gatherers. Admitting this, the population must have been exceedingly small. Despite a relative abundance and variety of game and fish, this bleak, rocky, and heavily wooded territory could support only tiny scattered groups, call them families or clans. The societies thus revealed might have remained—and, for all the relics they have left, did remain—static and petrified for centuries, nay for millennia. Historically, the way of progress and the possibility of supporting a larger population lay in the cultivation of wheat and barley and the breeding of horned cattle, sheep, and pigs.

Now, no wild grass native to the British Isles was waiting our Mesolithic gatherers' attention to turn into an edible cereal. It is most unlikely that sheep for taming and breeding roamed Scottish or Welsh hills. The Mesolithic inhabitants of Scotland would then have lacked the opportunity of progressing by their own motion along the historically determined path. A few ox-bones from the MacArthur Cave (Oban) and one sheep bone from the midden of Cnoc Sligeach, Oransay, indeed hint at the possibility that the Obanian hunters were turning into pastoralists. Such a development cannot be absolutely excluded—if only because of the notorious difficulty of proving a negative. On the available archaeological evidence and for the zoological and botanical grounds just stated it is most unlikely. It cannot be unMarxian to assert that the first cultivated plants and domestic food animals were brought to Scotland and brought, not by the winds or waves, but by actual human cultivators and herdsmen who came and settled on our soil. Such have stamped on the archaeological record the very definite impression of mature and highly developed technical and ceremonial traditions (expressed conspicuously for instance in pottery and in funerary architecture) of which no rudiments are perceptible in stage I. On the other hand at least Tardenoisean societies survived, preserving their old technical methods and presumably their food-gathering economy side by side with newcomers long enough to be able to imitate in their traditional technique some of the newcomers' devices such as tanged and barbed arrow-heads.

Some of the scattered bands of Mesolithic gatherers may have joined the immigrant farmers or copied their way of life, acquiring grains and stock. In the latter case they would multiply as a result of the increased regularity of the food-supply. Some recruitment from Mesolithic stocks in stages II and III seems in any case likely. Some of the bone-work from Skara Brae and even Jarlshof illustrates a survival of North Sea-Baltic traditions carried over from stage I. But no such survival is recognizable in the equipment of the most representative society in stage II, the Megalith-builders.

The nuclei of these would seem, from the distribution of their monuments, to have arrived by sea on the western coasts. At least, round the Solway and the Clyde, the typology of the tombs may illustrate the actual course of the colonization. Allegedly early tombs, preserving semicircular forecourts at the covering cairns' wider end, occur mainly on the coast near handy landfalls adjacent to isolated patches of easily cultivable land. Reputedly late and degenerate tombs alone penetrate deeper into the hinterland. But too few tombs have been excavated profitably for a reconstruction of the process of colonization to be reliable; the classification of tombs as early or late depends on *a priori* theories. Instead of embarking again on such speculations, I propose this time to describe the observable activities of the several societies as they appear already established on our coasts and islands.

Of these, two at least—the Megalithic and Skara Brae—contrasted in their whole way of life as much as in their ceramic art, have to be distinguished. It is not altogether inconceivable that the latter should have grown out of the former in response to appropriate internal and environmental pressures. But in default of any positive evidence for the transition, the two societies must be described separately. For convenience I shall invert their chronological and stadial order.

SKARA BRAE

The whole life of Neolithic society is revealed with such an unique wealth of detail in the miraculously preserved domestic sites of Skara Brae[1] and Rinyo[2] that a description of stage II can begin most conveniently there, albeit at the cost of a departure from the strictly chronological order. Moreover, though mostly later in time, the Skara Brae culture is, in many respects, more archaic, stadially earlier, more typically Neolithic than is the Megalithic.

The basis of life was in the first instance stockbreeding. Skara

---

[1] Childe, *Skara Brae.*   [2] *Proc. Soc. Ant., Scot.*, lxxiii, 6–31.

Brae lies on the edge of a grass-grown sandy tract that still provides ideal grazing. Well-drained moors, sloping up from Rinyo towards Faraclett Head, again afford good pasture, while even better grass would once have covered the Sourin valley below that is now under cultivation. Enormous quantities of bones from sheep and cattle, found all through the immense midden deposit, on the house floors and even in a bed at Skara Brae, show the importance in the villagers' diet of mutton and beef or rather veal. Professor Watson commented on the very high proportion of immature animals among the cattle bones submitted to him. 'It is of course due to the difficulty of providing winter forage to allow all, or even a large proportion of, the calves to be carried on until the grass grew again in the spring.' The same phenomenon is noticeable in other phases of Scottish prehistory wherever data are adequate.

The proportion of sheep to cattle also struck Watson as high. Though the selected bones submitted to him may not be a true random sample, his conclusion is surely reliable. Really, sheep are easier to raise under Scottish conditions and to that extent a more suitable stock for relatively ill-equipped and ignorant herdsmen.

The cattle were butchered with a blow on the forehead from a blunt and heavy instrument. Whether cows or ewes were milked is uncertain. Some of the pots from Rinyo would do quite well for milk bowls, but may just as well have served other purposes. Watson maintains that some bulls were castrated. On comparative evidence this advance in animal husbandry is quite compatible with the general level of culture manifested in the Orkney villages.

A few bones of swine were identified by Watson, but they were very rare and might have belonged to wild animals. As the selection submitted to him was chosen with a view to defining the varieties of animal represented at Skara Brae and not their relative numbers, the pig bones identified are likely to be disproportionately prominent. I believe that all belonged to wild swine whose tusks were also found.

Funnily enough there is no evidence at all for agriculture. No grains were preserved, but the sherds from Skara Brae have not been carefully scrutinized for casts. No trace of sickle gloss was detected on any of the many flints from Rinyo. No querns turned up at either site. Stone mortars, like modern 'knocking stanes', were common in both villages, but they could have been used for pounding other things than grain; one is said to have contained pounded fish-bones. Food production in the Skara Brae economy meant essentially stock-breeding.

Naturally the produce of this Neolithic activity was supplemented by a continuance of gathering activities of Palaeolithic origin. In particular, limpets were assiduously collected; their shells are everywhere at Skara Brae and a disused gallery was found blocked with sackloads of them. Fishing seems to have been curiously neglected in this insular economy. Fish-bones were noted by the earlier excavators of Skara Brae, but I hardly noticed any, whereas they are obtrusively conspicuous under similar soil conditions on Viking sites in Caithness and Shetland. No fishing tackle in the form of hooks, spears, or harpoons, was manufactured, while only two or three atypical stone objects from Skara Brae are even suggestive of net-sinkers. The bones of whales and seals were certainly utilized and doubtless their flesh devoured, but that does not prove pursuit of either mammal on the sea; a couple of accidentally stranded whales would account for all the cetacean bone recovered. Skara Brae was certainly located on the shore as were two other probable sites on Mainland, but Rinyo is as inland a site as could well be found on Rousay.

Red deer existed in Orkney, but their pursuit does not seem to have been organized as a source of food. Apart from the stag consumed by a party of refugees after the great storm that demolished house 7, hardly any deer bones were found at Skara Brae. Antlers were freely used in industry, but four out of six examined by Professor Watson, were shed antlers 'which must have been picked up as raw material'. No unmistakable hunting implements—arrow-heads or sling-stones—figure among the varied equipment collected at Skara Brae and Rinyo. So in the economy food-production outweighed food-gathering as in early Neolithic sites in Switzerland and the Danube basin.

For the provision of shelter, the stone houses embalmed in sand at Skara Brae illustrate a most ingenious adaptation to the physical environment, a cunning utilization of limited local resources and an astonishingly high standard of convenience and comfort. At Rinyo the dwellings nestled under the lee of a low cliff; at Skara Brae they may have been built in a trough between dunes. The walls were built of slabs of the local Caithness flag-stone laid horizontally and two courses deep. More effectually to exclude the unintermittent cold winds in the third architectural phase at Skara Brae, a packing of dung, peat ash, and sand 8 to 10 ft. thick, was heaped up round the walls and supported by a revetment or casing wall one skin deep. Eventually, in the fourth phase, all the space between dwellings was filled up with a similar packing which was even continued over the roofed alleys joining the houses so that the lanes became tunnels, as in an ants' nest. At Rinyo, dwellings were partly sunk into the scree from the cliff, but the principle of an artificial packing supported by a revetment seems to have been adopted on the downhill side.

The dwellings themselves (Fig. 3) are parallelograms with rounded corners varying in size from 21 ×20 to 15 ×11 ft. internally. A few feet above the floor the walls begin to corbel inwards, very slightly near the centres, more emphatically at the corners, where the overhang may be as much as 2 ft. 9 in., 9½ ft. above the floor. The apartments must accordingly have been relatively lofty, but when and how they were roofed is unknown. Though strictly one-roomed, every dwelling boasted from one to four cellular annexes in the walls—either round, 4 ft. 6 in. in diameter on the floor and corbelled over after some 4 feet, or tunnel-like, some 4 feet square and lintelled 3½ feet above the floor. Each apartment with its annexes formed a self-contained unit, entered by its own low narrow door that could be blocked by a stone slab secured on the inside by a stone bar sliding in holes cut in the stone jambs. The doorway was of course kept low deliberately to keep in the warm air that ascends.

Each one-roomed dwelling was commodiously furnished. The floor was composed of laid clay, supplemented by paving slabs of slatey flag. Heat and light were provided by a peat fire burning on a square hearth, bounded by flags on edge and generally provided with a fire back formed of an upright block. At Rinyo, at least, a clay oven, measuring over all some 2 ×2¼ ft., stood on a slab beside the hearth. On either side of the hearth against the wall was a bed fixed to the floor and framed by thin slabs on edge with stone bedposts at the outer corners to support some sort of canopy. The right-hand bed is always the larger, varying from 6½ ×3½ to 5 ×2¾ ft., while the corresponding left-hand beds measure respectively 5½ to 4½ ft. in length. In some habitations, at least, a third and still smaller bed enclosure was built against the front wall beside the doorway.

Above each bed, ambries or keeping-places were let into the side walls while against the rear wall were two tiers of stone

FIG. 3. PLANS OF DWELLINGS 7 AND 8 SKARA BRAE, ORKNEY

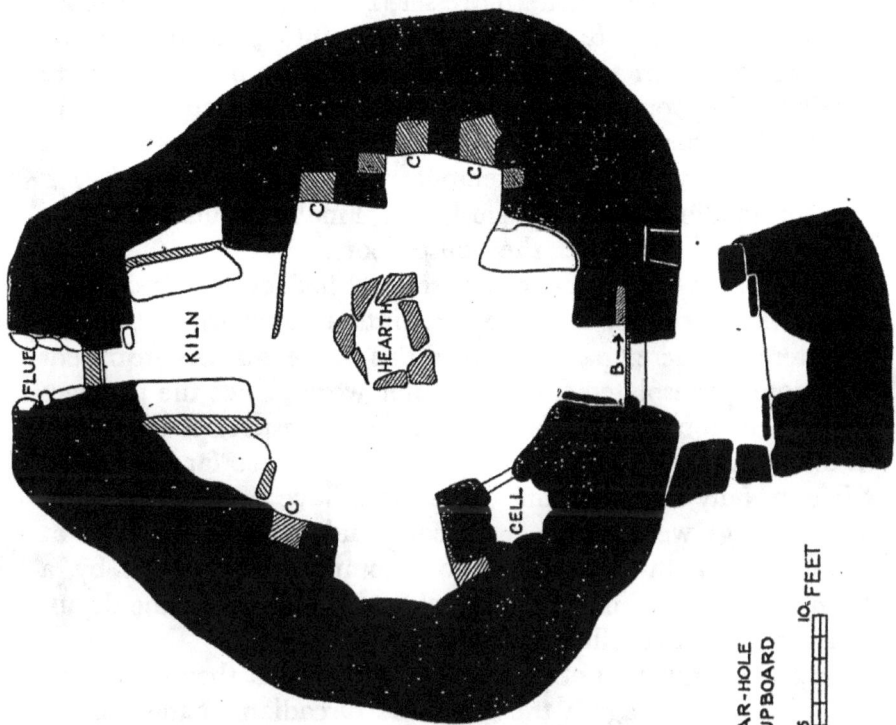

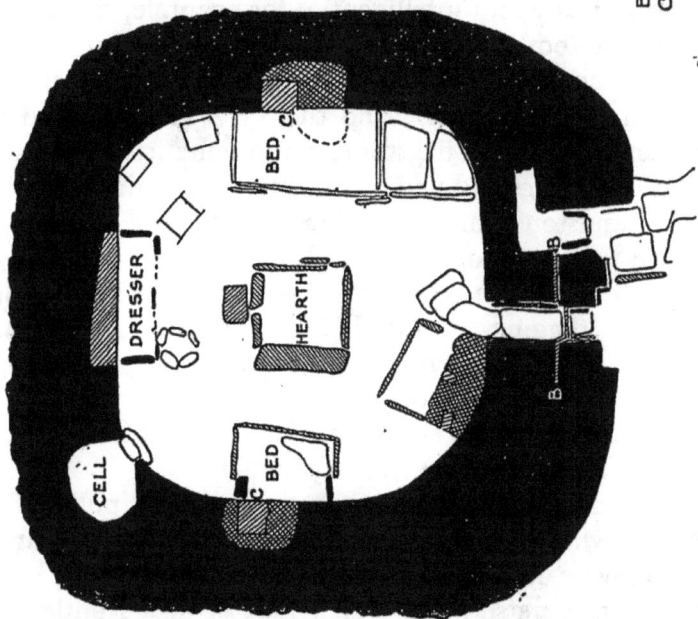

B = BAR-HOLE
C = CUPBOARD

0   5   10 FEET

shelves built just like a modern dresser (Plate II, 1). Of course all these constructions are just translations into stone under the exigencies of life on a treeless island of furniture made elsewhere of split saplings or planks. The compulsory immortalization in stone of Neolithic furniture in Orkney justifies the admission that more fortunately situated contemporaries may have enjoyed even more commodious wooden furnishings. Finally drains with stone sides and roofs ran under the house floors.

The self-contained units just described had been linked up at least by the last phase at Skara Brae into a larger whole through the system of covered passages. And this whole, like its constituent parts, could be isolated from the outer world, since the passages terminate in doors (Plate III, 1) similar in all respects to those that cut off individual dwellings. In the small area so far uncovered at Rinyo, only short sections of passages have been exposed but two dwellings were joined by a communication door. Both at Rinyo and Skara Brae the whole complex was served by a common system of built drainage-channels into which the drains from the several dwellings debouched.

For the instruments of production with which they controlled their environment again the Neolithic Orcadians made full use of local materials. They had evidently explored the neighbourhood systematically and intelligently; for example, a lump of the striking 'horse-tooth rock', a nodular concretion found at Yescenaby some four miles across the hills to the south-west, had been carried to Skara Brae. And there the villagers used clays, selected varieties of local flagstone, camptonite from the frequent volcanic dykes, chert and nodular haematite obtainable from the Old Red Sandstone formations, and bone and antler. Flint pebbles are very rare on Orkney Mainland and relatively few flints were used at Skara Brae; only forty-five flakes were collected in three years' digging. A poor black chert was used instead, no less than 125 pieces being recovered. On Rousay, however, flint pebbles are fairly common on the beaches; no less than 250 flint implements, together with eighty split but unworked pebbles, were picked up in a single season at Rinyo.

For chopping the villagers were provided with polished stone axes, though what they chopped therewith is far from clear. The smaller axes were attached to their handles, not directly, but with the aid of a transversely perforated haft of deer's antler into a hollowed end of which the axe was inserted. An astonishing skill in stone working is displayed in a remarkable series of balls and other objects of hard volcanic stone carved with spikey knobs and ridges in high relief. The carving must have been done with the aid of sand as an abrasive, but the function of the products is quite unknown.

The scarcity of flint made the provision of knives difficult. At Skara Brae the trouble was ingeniously surmounted by splitting beach pebbles along their bedding planes; by simply dashing one against a rock you can detach an oval flake which if neither very sharp nor at all durable could easily be replaced. Small scrapers were made of chert at Skara Brae, or flint at Rinyo. These, together with a variety of heavy bone tools, some of which look like adzes, were most likely used in dressing hides. A multitude of bone awls or borers and a few bodkins were presumably employed for perforating the hides and sewing them together for garments. No spindle whorls nor other textile appliances have been recognized. Presumably then the villagers wore skins. Stout bone and ivory pins suitable for fastening such, as well as toggles, have been found, but no buttons.

Pots of considerable size were built up by hand from successive rings and sometimes tastefully decorated. But excessively big grits were left in the clay, and the peat fuel failed to provide sufficient heat to convert more than a superficial skin into pottery. Vessels were also made of sandstone and whales' vertebra.

For this equipment the villagers were emphatically self-sufficing. No imported materials were found either at Skara Brae or Rinyo. The extreme rarity of flint at the former site when a kindred community on a neighbouring island drew freely on a local supply illustrates the extent to which this Neolithic independence was carried.

Nor is there conclusive evidence for division of labour between the several households within the community. There stood indeed outside the main complex of interconnected dwellings at Skara Brae an isolated building, No. 8 (Fig. 3), which might be interpreted as the residence of an artisan family. Chips of chert littering the floor and five bone implements with blunted ends, interpreted as fabricators, prove that knapping was conducted there. The rear end of the structure was occupied by an ingenious kiln, beside which was a store of clay; though no wasters were found, the kiln may have served for pot-firing. On the other hand, the structure comprised a normal central hearth with pillared back, and there were recesses like beds on either side with keeping-places in their back walls (Plate II, 2). Yet these recesses were not partitioned off like the usual beds, the kiln occupies the space where the dresser should stand, and there are no slate boxes let into the floor, and unusually little food refuse upon it. Hence the essential items of domestic furniture are missing and the building, as found (it had undergone some reconstruction), does not seem to have been used as a dwelling.

Perhaps, then, it was not the dwelling of a family of artisans who worked for the whole community, but had been turned into a communal workshop where members of the several households manufactured the tools and vessels they required. In general, then, we may say the members of each household made the individual articles they used and owned individually. At the same time, in making pots at the communal kiln (if such it were), the women from various houses would doubtless help one another.

Even so, this simple pastoral economy entailed social relations; it could only function through the continuous and organized co-operation of all its beneficiaries. This co-operation finds concrete expression in the archaeological record in obviously communal works—the paved and covered streets, the common drains, a paved open space or square. If individual households might theoretically build their own houses as well as make their own tools, these structures jointly used must have been built co-operatively. How was this co-operation achieved?

The individual dwellings should correspond to individual families. On ethnographic analogies we should expect these to be patriarchal in such a pastoral community, and one scrap of concrete evidence points that way too. At Skara Brae and Rinyo the right-hand bed in every house is the larger. Now in a Highland 'black house' last century the right-hand side of the single room was the men's side, the left reserved for women. This convention may very well be an insular survival of the Neolithic tradition. But a black house, of course, housed a patriarchal family. So should its Stone Age precursor.

The several houses, as has been said, differed in size. But there is no difference in plan or the kind of furniture. In other words, there are no positive indications of differences in rank, nothing like a chief's palace. The organization of co-operative activity by a Leader seems unlikely; the communities appear equalitarian.

On the other hand, the whole plan of these Orcadian villages concretely reflects a very compact social organization. If Skara Brae be from one point of view a cluster of six one-roomed houses, from another it is a single six-roomed house. Physically, the six apartments, if not exactly under one roof, are at least under one midden; a resident could pass from one to another along the tortuous alleys without going into the fresh air. This arrangement seems to be an unusually clear archaeological counterpart of a familiar conception of society; its members were members of one enlarged household and considered themselves as related members of a single great family—a clan. Consequently within the whole group tasks were apportioned and their performance ensured by the same unformulated rules and sanctions as hold within a modern family.

With such a sociological structure there are neither ruling nor exploited classes and the land at least is communally owned. As long as the principal means of production—in this instance flocks and herds—are likewise held in common, we have 'primitive communism' in the Marxian sense; this does not preclude private property in articles individually made and used, such as tools and ornaments. In default of evidence for private ownership of stock, such as is forthcoming by stage IV at least, we may provisionally assume that primitive communism still reigned at Skara Brae and Rinyo, though personal possessions in the form of gear, clothing, and ornaments are implied by the keeping-places over the beds and the hoards of beads found in some cells.

Of the ideological lubricants that kept this social mechanism running smoothly we have curiously little evidence. Two old women had been buried under the wall of one dwelling at Skara Brae. That may imply a belief that a ghost was needed to hold up a wall—a widespread superstition perfectly compatible with the low stage of technological development exemplified in the village. On the other hand, the absence of any room or structure suggestive of a shrine or a temple may be significant. Magic powers and ghosts would have been recognized, but gods no more than chiefs.

For the rest we know the villagers adorned walls, pots, and implements with geometrical patterns, painted their bodies red, yellow, and white, and hung round their persons strings of beads and pendants made from bone, cows' teeth, and walrus ivory. They played games with dice and knuckle-bones.

In the sequel we should expect that ownership of stock will pass from the clan to the separate constituent families, thus weakening, without completely destroying, the former's solidarity. Though Skara Brae and Rinyo themselves disappear and the society they represent become merged in a wider whole—the

3

ceramic traditions of Rinyo are still recognizable in the pottery from Eday of stage VIa—the subsequent evidence will justify these expectations. But we must first examine the other societies representative of stage II.

THE MEGALITHIC SOCIETY

It is much less easy to define the economy of the Megalith-builders; for no actual dwellings and only two domestic sites are known. Since one of these was situated on the slopes of Wideford Hill just below tomb 67, it may be assumed that the tombs, which are our main source of information, were located beside or over-looking the settlements. In Rousay[1] each tomb corresponds to a natural agricultural unit, generally still or till recently farmed by a community and comprising in each case a stream, a strip of good arable land below, and a tract of pasture above the tomb. Round the Firth of Clyde and Loch Fyne, again, each tomb overlooks a strip of raised beach terrace or alluvial soil that can be easily cultivated and usually still is. In the valleys of the Beauly, the Nairn, and the Spey the Clava tombs are con-spicuously confined to recent alluvia that are at least fairly well drained, and the same is true of the isolated tombs in Strath Earn and Glen Almond. Even in Caithness a typical cemetery like that on Warehouse Hill dominates the fertile ground around the Loch of Yarrows.

All this suggests mixed farming. Grain-growing is, in fact, directly attested for the Clyde group by querns, approximating to the typical saddle type, from the settlement at Townhead, Rothesay. On the other hand, in the interior of Galloway and southern Ayrshire some Solway tombs are located on high moors that are to-day barren swamps and must always have been more suitable for grazing or hunting than for grain-growing.

For other groups stock-breeding is amply attested by the bones found in the tombs themselves. Bones of cattle have been identi-fied from ten tombs (33, 37, 38, 87, 111, 112, 113, 300, 301, 311),[2] of sheep from six (33, 37, 38, 87, 300, 301), and of pig from five (113, 115, 300, 301, 311). A disproportionate number of the cattle bones belong to immature beasts, as at Skara Brae, and for the same reason. Judging from the funeral meats, in Arran cattle-raising was more important than sheep-breeding, whereas in Orkney the sheep bones preponderate numerically; in Caith-ness they are curiously rare. On the other hand, pig bones are

---

[1] *Ant. J.*, xxii, p. 139.   [2] Numbers refer to list in Appendix.

missing altogether in Orkney, but occur in Caithness and are
prominent in Arran, actually outnumbering cattle bones in 300.

Hunting seems to have played a much more important role in
the food quest of the Megalith-builders than at Skara Brae.
Bones of red deer and wild fowl are prominent in the tombs of
all areas, but especially in Caithness and Orkney. In 113 and 37
red deer were absolutely the commonest animals, no less than
thirty individuals being represented in 37. In two Caithness
tombs (111, 112) bones of horses are reported as the principal
items surviving from the funeral feast. The beasts thus used for
food were probably wild. The arrows found in so many tombs
may be regarded as huntsman's tools buried with their owners.
Similarly, canine bones from six tombs (37, 87, 111, 112, 113, 300)
most probably mean that the departed huntsman took his dog
with him.

Being a maritime folk the Megalith-builders might have been
expected to increase their diet by fishing, but it is only in Orkney
(33) that fish-bones have actually been recorded in a tomb.
Shell-fish were collected in Caithness too (37, 87), and birds' eggs
at least in Orkney (33).

The relative prominence of hunting would seem to give the
Megalithic economy a more archaic aspect than that of Skara
Brae. The impression is illusory. The stratigraphical evidence
from the Swiss lake-dwellings and Danubian sites in Central
Europe shows that in temperate Europe hunting became pro-
gressively more important during the Neolithic stage—the direct
reverse of what would be expected by *a priori* theorists, and is
observed in Egypt and Iran. This development is really a proper
response to environmental conditions in the temperate zone as
Krichevskiï[1] was the first to note. Here, with the rudimentary
agricultural science and equipment at first available, an economy
based on hunting and on farming with emphasis on pastoralism
yields an easier return than a predominantly agricultural one—
within, of course, very narrow limits.

For the rest the Megalith-builders, judging by the tools surviving and their products, were no better equipped technologically
than the inhabitants of Skara Brae and Rinyo. But their economy
appears more progressive inasmuch as it was less narrowly self-
sufficing than what we have just learned to know in Orkney.
The most direct evidence of this is the quite extensive use of flint,
proved not only by the regular deposition of flint implements in

---

[1] *Izvestiya GAIMK*, 100 (1933), 175 ff.

the tombs, but also by the large numbers of such implements that have been collected around the tombs, and in particular on the domestic site of Wideford Hill. To accumulate such quantities collection over extensive areas and in some instances inter-communal exchange must be presumed. In fact the flint used in Arran was imported from Antrim, as in stage I in Kintyre. At the same time pitchstone,[1] a volcanic glass with all the good qualities of flint, was utilized not only in Arran, where it is native, but also in Bute (where pieces were found in tombs 295 and 297), and most probably in south-western Galloway and Ayrshire too.

The situation of tombs on little islands like Holm of Papa Westray and the Calf of Eday shows conclusively that the Megalith-builders were mariners. Round the Clyde the tombs overlook fertile tracts at the head of bays hemmed in on the landward side by rugged hills, dense forests, and forbidding swamps, so that their builders must have arrived by sea. In fact, despite fierce and frequent tempests, the firths and sounds offer enticing oppor-tunities for maritime intercourse.

The remarkable uniformity in funerary architecture and ceramic art not only all round Loch Fyne and the Firth of Clyde, but also across the North Channel to Ulster and even to Man must reflect the utilization of these opportunities. It demonstrably resulted in an interchange of materials—flint—and presumably also of ideas. A single culture ruled round the North Channel. Its unity can only have been maintained by interchange of visits at however long intervals. The similar cultural uniformi-ties observable in the Orkney archipelago, and even on both sides of the Pentland Firth and along the north-west coast of the Moray Firth must be interpreted in the same manner. We may picture these grey seas as bright with Neolithic Argonauts as the western Pacific is to-day. The attested or inferential interchange of goods and ideas did not indeed on the available evidence develop into a regular and organized commerce in necessities

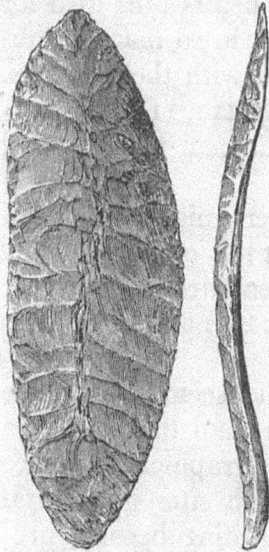

FIG. 4. PLANO-CONVEX (SLUG) KNIFE OF ANTRIM FLINT FROM GIANTS' GRAVES, ARRAN. $\frac{2}{3}$

---

[1] *Proc.*, lii, 142; xxxviii, 77; and xliii, 369.

within stage II. It doubtless prepared the way for that development in stage III.

There are indeed some hints of intercommunal specialization. On the tiny islet, Eilean an Tighe, on the inland Loch nan Geireann in North Uist, Sir Lindsay Scott[1] identified the dilapidated remains of two pottery kilns used consecutively over a considerable period. Enormous quantities of sherds and wasters littered the site. The output of the kilns must have exceeded the demands of any community that could dwell on the islet or even round the loch; the products must have been exported to a wider market, the extent of which cannot yet be estimated. Vases of Unstan ware from Orkney, so like some sherds from Eilean an Tighe as to suggest fabrication there, prove on petrological examination to have been made in all likelihood from local clay in Orkney; so trade in pots between different archipelagos is unproven. Probably intercommunal division of labour in stage II was just incipient; for intracommunal specialization there is no more evidence than at Skara Brae.

Nevertheless, as much as there, each local group of Megalith-builders formed a co-operating unit. The most spectacular archaeological result of this co-operation is the chambered cairn itself—a stupendous work that could only be accomplished by a substantial labour force. The organization of the social unit has to be deduced from the tomb and its furniture. Now, as remarked in most areas, each tomb or cemetery corresponds to a geographical unit that would naturally be occupied by a group of farmers. But who were buried in such tombs?

Every excavated tomb contained the remains of several individuals, though the precise number could be determined only in a few cases. The maxima recorded are 29 in Orkney (37), 30 in Caithness (112), and 14 in Arran (301). The average for 11 tombs is 12, but 5 contained not more than 3 skeletons. The largest tombs do not contain the most corpses; on the contrary, only 2 were detected in 38, though it is much larger than 37, and on Arran 301 with its 14 skeletons is only half the size of 300, which contained but 8. Admittedly the entrances are normally found to have been carefully blocked up and deliberately hidden. Yet the Scottish evidence now proves, what had been inferred from analogies elsewhere, that the tombs were in fact used for successive burials over a considerable time; the undertakers must have possessed traditional knowledge of the well-concealed

---

[1] *Man*, 1939, p. 25; *Proc.*, lxxvi, 130.

entrance and on each occasion have removed the blocking from the passage or portal. The tombs were, in fact, communal ossuaries or family vaults used for several generations. The crucial question is: was such a chambered cairn erected as the burial-place of a line of local chiefs and their families or to house the remains of all members of the local group?

The alternatives are not, of course, strictly exclusive. On the Marne, for instance, we know systadial collective tombs some of which, containing only a few skeletons but rich grave goods, must have been reserved for chiefs, while others of similar plan but less elaborate contain poor grave goods, but a hundred or so skeletons presumably of commoners. In Scotland, save perhaps in some Caithness cemeteries, no such contrast can be detected and the question cannot be escaped.

On the answer to this question depend not only our conception of the course of social development, but also our estimate of the total population. It could be settled objectively only by the discovery and total excavation of a settlement connected with a tomb. There may perhaps still be hopes of such around Loch Fyne. In the interval we can only rely on inconclusive theoretical and comparative arguments. On the one hand, in stage VI, the prehistoric castles of the same Highland regions seem to indicate a society divided into chiefs and retainers, while the finest foreign parallels to our Neolithic vaults—the beehive tombs or *tholoi* of Mycenaean Greece—were certainly 'royal tombs'. On the other hand, the Copper Age or Early Bronze Age chamber tombs of Cyprus, the Cyclades, Early Minoan Crete, Siculan I, and Los Millares in south-eastern Spain, which in plan and ritual offer the closest analogies to the Scottish monuments, were used by families or clans without regard to rank.

I shall assume that each chambered cairn was the communal burying-place of a clan or enlarged family of the same kind and size as we have learned to know from the systadial Orkney villages. Such a group would be large enough to provide the man-power to build even a long cairn given several years to complete the operation. On this assumption the chambered cairn is the symbol of a clan society and primitive communism in the sense defined above.

Though in a pastoral society cattle raiding provides an economic inducement to warfare, the primary grave goods at least afford no explicit evidence for bellicose behaviour (arrow-heads are to be regarded as huntsman's tools while the mace-heads (Fig. 5) belonging to types recurring in English graves of stage IV may be attributed to late secondary interments). On the other hand, it would be an anachronism to deduce any formal political organization of the clans from the observed regional uniformities in sepulchral architecture and ceramic style. Such might merely reflect communities of tradition reinforced by interchange of friendly visits and very likely intermarriage. Nor do the wider communities of funerary architecture and ritual between Scotland and other parts of the British Isles and Atlantic Europe in general

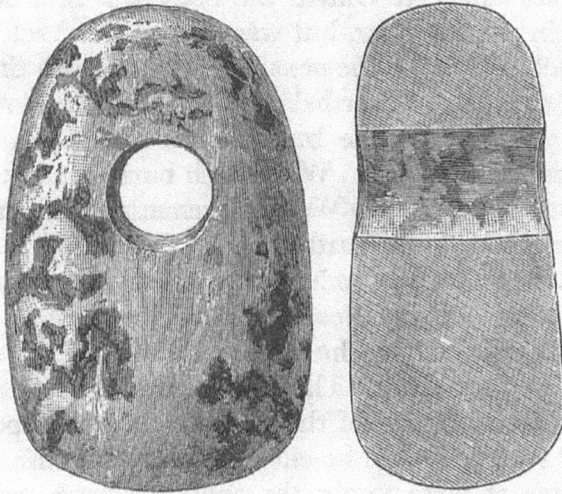

FIG. 5. MACE-HEAD FROM CHAMBERED CAIRN, TORMORE, ARRAN. $\frac{2}{3}$

justify the deduction of a common religious institution or church. They must indicate a fundamental unity of beliefs and practices of the ideological superstructure appropriate to the Megalithic-Neolithic economy.

The general nature of this superstructure is plain—a reverence for and fear of the dead, presumably as powers that control or influence the weather, the crops, the fertility of herds, and the general health and prosperity of society. Such an attitude is almost universal to-day among sedentary barbarians, though its expression varies widely. Among our ancestors it inspired the erection of a monumental tomb after elaborate ceremonies, the ceremonial deposition of the departed to the accompaniment of rites that involved the kindling of fire in the tomb, the surrender to the defunct of part at least of his or her gear and the provision of meats even at the cost of the slaughter of part of the community's capital in livestock.

Nothing attests further tendence, still less worship. On the contrary, in the sequel to make room for a new corpse the bones of previous burials were often unceremoniously pushed aside or even trampled underfoot. Sometimes they were singed or charred by the great fire that formed part of every funeral. Anderson and Greenwell describe masses of incinerated human bones on the chamber floors in Caithness and Argyll, but the 'incineration' may well have been accidental. The latest interments were nearly always found unburnt, in their natural articulation and in the contracted attitude. At Unival the body was first deposited in a small cist in the chamber, but was removed and set against the chamber wall in time for the next funeral, by which time the skin would have decayed. Nevertheless in Bute (298) and Arran (304, 312), as in Ulster, genuine burials after cremation have been found in chambered cairns. While such burials may conceivably be synchronous with the Wessex cremations of stage IV in southern England, it is hardly likely that Clyde society had progressed so far; in 304 some pottery was appropriate to III, that from 298 exclusively Neolithic Beacharra ware.

I have remarked above how some Solway tombs spread out on to the high moorlands. That would indicate an emphasis on the hunting-pastoral side of the economy at the expense of the agricultural such as would be encouraged by Scottish conditions. Now, in some of these tombs the chambers have grown rather small and the passages have become symbolic. Thus, in the King's Cairn, Water of Deugh (342) the chambers measure 6 ft. 6 in. × 2 ft. 6 in. and 7 ft. × 2 ft. 6 in. respectively, while the 'entrance passages', though 17 and 22 ft. long, are so low and narrow that they can hardly have been actually used for the introduction of successive interments. Such chambers, in fact, can hardly have served as collective tombs at all. So, too, some Clyde tombs (291, 292, 297) have been reduced to a single modest compartment. And then in Argyll above Crinan two round cairns covered each a central cist, no larger than a normal short cist, but connected on the east with a crescentic setting of uprights[1] which, though completely buried in the mass of the cairn, preserves the form of the façade appropriate to a Clyde horned cairn. Here we see the collective tombs turning into an individual sepulchre. Similarly, while the classical and presumably oldest Clava tombs were entered by a distinct passage, there are some that are completely closed and lack any entrance. Such

[1] *Proc.*, lxiv, 139.

can hardly have been collective tombs used for successive interments.

Now we have taken the collective tombs as symbolic of a social unit organized on a kinship basis, a clan, and owning the means of production in common. But among barbarian pastoralists to-day we find a tendency for the ownership of flocks and herds to pass into the hands of individual patriarchal families. The replacement of collective by individual burial may be one symptom of consequence of this emergence of the pairing family as an independent economic unit.

This tends to weaken the solidarity of the clan; the several individual families may scatter with their beasts for part of the year at least or even disperse completely like Abraham and Lot.

Moreover, I have suggested that the chambered cairn expresses the belief that the ancestral spirits are collectively responsible for the prosperity of the clan and the fertility of its herds and crops. If now this collective potence be absorbed by an individual who by reason of age or success in magic, war, or practical life acquires authority, he becomes a 'divine king', his ghost concentrates the magic power of the whole clan, and his tomb becomes the clan shrine instead of the collective tomb sacred to the clans' ancestors as a whole. The Recumbent Stone Circles of Aberdeenshire that typologically are descended from the Clava tombs, may ideologically be the result of some such process of development.

But Recumbent Stone Circles pretty certainly belong to stage IV. In speculating on the course of social development I have anticipated the order of events. Historically the developments adumbrated did not take place without the stimulus of an invasion. The Beaker folk who in the archaeological record appear as the pioneers of individual interment in Scotland acted as catalysts, accelerating a change that was indeed logically necessary but that might have been indefinitely postponed.

CHAPTER III

THE EARLY BRONZE AGE

BEAKER folk who released the immanent forces of social change
were immigrants, foreign to the British Isles; for they differ quite
conspicuously in physical characters from the population represented in our chamber tombs and from the old women found
under the walls of Skara Brae. And economic changes alone could
hardly alter cranial shape so decisively and so swiftly.

But though an actual invasion must be admitted, it did not
wipe out the older population, annihilate established societies,
nor suppress their distinctive cultures. As already remarked,
Beaker pottery, distinctive of the invaders, has been found in ten
of the thirty-five chambers successfully excavated; round-headed
skulls of the invader's type have been found in other tombs. This
must mean that some of the invaders secured by intermarriage,
adoption, or how you will, admission to the clan whose members
were alone rightfully entitled to burial in the communal vault.
In some tombs (87, 297), indeed, sherds of more than one Beaker
were found betokening more than one interment after the invasion.
But as a rule the Beaker burials are the last. Even in the Megalithic province, subsequent interments are usually individual
burials in short cists sometimes inserted into the cairn already
covering the collective tomb, sometimes covered by a new round
cairn built beside the old one (for instance, at Camster and near
Kenny's Cairn in Caithness). The new rite of individual burial
—with all the implications set forth above—eventually took the
place of collective burial in the new composite society.

The relations between Beaker-folk and the people of Skara Brae
are not so clearly defined. At Rinyo nothing in the context of
the single Beaker found in a secondary floor of a dwelling pointed
to a violent destruction nor an abrupt abandonment of the site.
Near Gullane and North Berwick Beaker sherds and Skara Brae
sherds occur side by side in the same middens. In north-east
Scotland the Skara Brae traditions of potting survived to reassert
themselves on the Encrusted Urns of stage V; in Eday they are
still recognizable in stage VIa. Probably Skara Brae people
persist to be incorporated in the society of stages III and IV.

At Hedderwick, near Dunbar, and on Glenluce Sands sherds

of Beaker, Western, and Peterborough wares apparently occur side by side. In any case, as already indicated, Callander's overlap pottery from the settlements near Muirkirk,[1] and Glenluce, and on the Forth coasts and from burials at Drumelzier,[2] Old Kilpatrick,[3] and Giants' Graves[4] is the ceramic symbol of fusion of traditions not of replacement. All this goes to show the incorporation of 'Neolithic' societies into the Bronze Age society of stage III.

Nothing in the funerary record warrants the presentation of the invading race as a class of overlords supported by the toil of 'Neolithic' serfs or clients. The simple and modestly furnished cists (Plate VI, 2), without any surviving cairn, that contain 72 per cent of the recorded Beaker burials, are not the least aristocratic. The six double interments in one cist cannot legitimately be explained as burials of slaves with master or mistress. In three instances both the deceased were equally well—or ill—furnished with funerary gifts. In two graves (189a and 191a), in which both defunct were of the same sex and much the same age, only one of the skeletons was accompanied by the usual funerary gift— a Beaker. But in each case both subjects belonged to the same round-headed, Beaker race.

Doubtless the racial distinctions which must have subsisted not only enriched society culturally and genetically, but also may have facilitated the rise of chieftainship, encouraged by other causes, and the concentration of a social surplus. But we cannot regard society of stage III as a class or stratified society of conquerors exploiting conquered.

Judged by the food refuse from the Lothian middens and grain imprints on pottery there discovered, the basis of the Beaker economy was much the same as that of the Megalithic culture. Beaker burials are concentrated in what is now the best agricultural land in the Tweed basin, the Lothians and north-east Scotland. On the west and north, their distribution tends to follow that of the Neolithic chambered cairns, but there are significant divergencies. Beaker graves or settlements have been found in Ardgour, in Mull, and round Ardnamurchan—regions poor in arable soils and eschewed by the Neolithic cultivators. In Ayrshire, too, settlements and graves spread on to the high moors round Muirkirk and between the Nith and Doon. This may indicate a greater interest in pastures and hunting-grounds than in cultivable land and the transition to a predominantly

[1] *Proc.*, lxi, 269.   [2] ibid., lxv, 366.   [3] ibid., lxiii, 37.   [4] ibid., xxxvii, 44.

pastoral economy to which Megalithic communities at least of the Solway group were also drifting.

Hunting and collecting were at least as important as with the Megalith builders. In the shore middens along the Forth the bones of deer and fish occur as well as those of sheep and kine, while whelk, limpet, snail, and oyster shells mingled with crabs' claws are abundant. The arrows, so commonly found in cists with beakers may be huntsmen's tools or warrior's arms, but a dog (8) would be an appropriate companion for a huntsman.

The ascertained remains of Beaker habitations are a couple of hut-circles on the moors near Muirkirk[1] and shallow middens on the coasts of the Lothians, Fife, Wigtownshire, Ayrshire, and the Western Isles. Similarly Beaker burials occur as a rule in isolated short cists containing a single skeleton and not grouped in cemeteries. Such monuments should belong to less sedentary communities than can be inferred from the spacious collective tombs of the Megalithic culture and stratified village sites like Skara Brae and Rinyo. They are, in fact, appropriate to the economy forecasted for stage III and symbolic of the dispersion of the clan anticipated as its correlative. They should belong to independent families, each owning their own little herd and ranging widely in search of pasture and game.

Technologically the Beaker culture, judged by grave goods and domestic rubbish, was no more advanced than those attributed to stage II; it was still essentially Neolithic. But economically it is at once contrasted with the Neolithic, not indeed by the use of metal, but by the frequence of imported materials. Even such a relatively early grave as the cist in the chamber under the long cairn at Yarrows (149a) contained a necklace of jet (lignite) beads; the material could not be obtained nearer than Brora on the opposite side of the Ord ridge and Helmsdale river. Lignite beads were associated with beakers in four other graves (8, 92, 194, 202a).

Flint seems to have been used more extensively than before and for the manufacture of larger objects that could hardly be made out of the small nodules usually available in Scotland. At Nunraw, East Lothian, there was discovered, not it is true in a grave but close to the site of the beaker cist (154a) discovered in 1944, a flint dagger $7\frac{1}{4}$ inches long.[2] It belongs to a type regularly associated with A Beakers in England and represented by smaller examples in Scotland from the Tweed basin and Angus.

[1] *Proc.*, xlviii, 373; liv, 210.   [2] *Proc.*, xxiii, 18.

FIG. 6. DISTRIBUTION OF BURIALS WITH BEAKERS

● C. Beaker
▲ B. Beaker

Similarly, on English analogies, large very thin axes with pointed butts made of choice stones,[1] preferably greenish, should belong to the Beaker complex; they, too, must be products of trade. Although—and perhaps because—dispersed, Beaker communities were less exclusively self-sufficing than those of stage II; they indulged in some sort of trade.

Eventually this trade brought them metal that was destined to release new forces of production. Objects of copper or bronze are indeed associated with beakers in only five graves (77, 90, 91, 228, 202a) and consist of weapons (knife-daggers) and ornaments. Moreover, the graves in question are so late that they may be regarded as systadial as well as synchronous with Food Vessel graves of stage IV. The use of bronze begins with the Beaker culture but so timidly that one is in doubt how far it should be assigned to stage III at all. The numerous flat axes for instance found in north-east Scotland, must have been used by Beaker folk. But, as we have seen, Beaker folk were the dominant element in society there during stage IV.

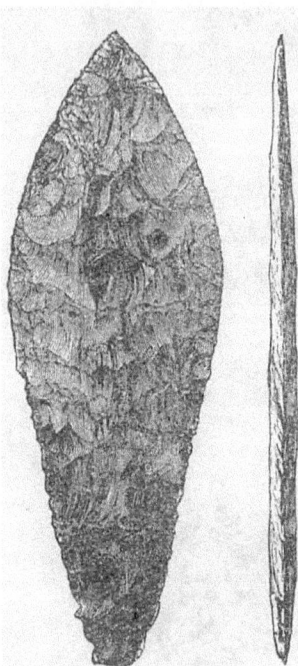

In stage III, in any case, trade was already so brisk that we may fairly speak of commodity production—the extraction or manufacture of articles for barter and not for use by the maker.

FIG. 7. FLINT DAGGER, NUNRAW, EAST LOTHIAN. ⅔

We may at least suspect intercommunal specialization of labour. North-east Scotland was provided with flint from the deposits of Buchan.[2] There along the crest of a ridge that runs for nearly eight miles from near Peterhead, south-west to the Hill of Dudwick, lies a rich bed of resorted flint nodules. Near Skelmuir and Boddam there occur on it circular depressions 45 to 55 feet in diameter and a couple of feet deep. In one pit over a thousand flint flakes and eighteen anvil-stones (Fig. 8) were found while other anvil-stones are to be picked up all round.[3] The pits are evidently monuments to communities of flint-workers, comparable to those of the South Downs and East Anglia, who

[1] *Proc.*, vi, 179; xvii, 382 f.; xxvi, 174; xxxii, 130; lxiv, 298.
[2] *Proc.*, xxx, 346–51.   [3] *P.S.E.A.*, iii (1918), 33–47; cf. *Proc.* li, 117 ff.

apparently produced flint as a commodity, exchanging it for food and other materials grown by contemporary communities. In view of the extensive use of flint by Beaker-folk it may be assumed that this exploitation was going on in stage III.

Metallurgy certainly involved specialization. Throughout Bronze Age Europe and Hither Asia the evidence is that smelting was done only on the ore fields since only there are slag heaps found. The product in barbarian Europe was purveyed by itinerant smiths who travelled with half-finished articles to be finished off to the taste of the purchaser. To Scotland the

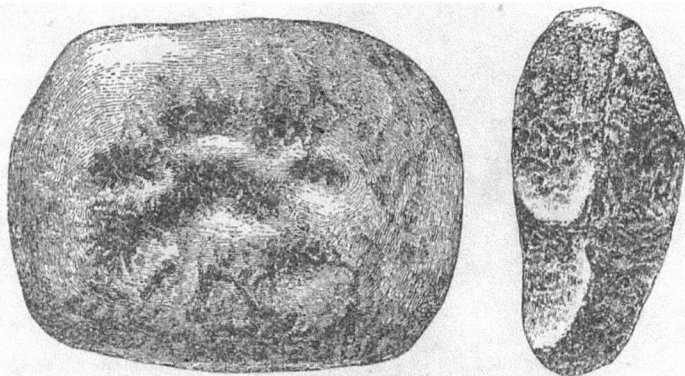

FIG. 8. ANVIL AND HAMMER-STONE, SKELMUIR, BUCHAN

merchant-artificers came from Ireland. There are no grounds for supposing that the secret of metallurgy was independently discovered in Scotland—for instance no correlation can be detected between early metal tools and copper lodes—nor yet that the Beaker folk arrived with bronze-smiths in tow. Most probably the material and the products too came from Ireland. Big concentrations of flat axes in Galloway and Ayrshire look like imports; a couple along the Great Glen, like unambiguously Irish halberds in stage IV, would mark the natural route for trade between Ireland and north-east Scotland. About eighteen are stamped as 'made in Ireland' by the patterns that adorn them; for such decorated axes are common only there.[1] Some flat axes were, however, cast here, as several stone moulds (Fig. 9) have been found round the Moray Firth and in the north-east. Such probably belong to stage IV and, even so, need not indicate resident smiths. The itinerant artisans presumably carried their tools as well as their materials with them.

Of course such specialization and commodity production

[1] *P.P.S.*, iv, 272–82.

pre-suppose the production of a social surplus. *Ex hypothesi* the flint-workers, metallurgists, and traders, did not grow or catch their own food. They obtained it by exchanging their goods for what the consuming societies produced over and above their own domestic needs. Such transactions were obviously simpler with separate ownership of herds than under the hypothetical régime of primitive communism. Metal weapons and ornaments are wanted by individuals for personal use, but can best be paid for in cattle or sheep that the purveyors could eat. But the individual

FIG. 9.   STONE MOULD FOR FLAT AXES, HILL OF FOUDLAND,
INSCH, ABERDEENSHIRE

member of a communistic clan could hardly buy articles of personal use with society's collectively owned capital. He could with his own.

On the other hand the surplus produced by an individual family above the requirements of domestic consumption is liable to have been exceedingly small under a rural economy so backward that a large proportion of each season's calves had simply to be eaten. For a community to acquire any substantial quantity of foreign material a concentration of the surplus would be requisite. Historical testimony from the Bronze Age civilizations of the Ancient East and ethnographic evidence from Polynesia and North America show that one way of effecting this concentration is the institution of chieftainship, another the cult of a deity. From voluntary customary gifts or free-will offerings made by each family of followers or votaries from its tiny surplus, the real chief or the representative of the imaginary god can accumulate quite a substantial surplus.

For such divine worship the archaeological record offers no conclusive evidence. The great Ring of Brodgar in Orkney should, on English evidence, be a sanctuary and should by the same token have been reared by Beaker folk. That does not mean it was a temple where offerings accumulated as in Mesopotamia. On the other hand the monumental cairns that cover a minority of Beaker graves and the circles of great stones that surround others look like chieftain's tombs. Like chambered cairns, their erection required the collective labour of a larger group than a single family. Like them they seem to be in a sense temples as well as tombs. But they are individual, not communal burial places.

At the same time chieftainship would help to solve the political problem raised by the itinerant artisan and trader. In barbarian society organized on a kinship basis, the person and goods of an individual are guaranteed by the support of his kinsmen, in the last resort by the blood feud. But an itinerant Irish copper-smith could count on no such protection. By no plausible fiction could he claim membership of a Scottish Beaker clan. Now his customers would naturally be only the rich, those who possessed an effective surplus, the largest flocks and herds. If such were armed with political authority, they could guarantee safe-conduct to their welcome visitors as well as purchasing their products.

How such political authority can be acquired is naturally a matter of guesswork. Besides mere seniority, practical success, real or reputed wisdom, prowess in war, may have helped. Cattle-raiding, as noted, offered a solid economic inducement to war. That the Beaker-folk succumbed seems highly probable. If the common flint arrow-heads be still merely huntsmen's tools, the flint and bronze daggers must surely be weapons of war. At Piekie in Fife,[1] a short cist contained a man of Beaker type (though not accompanied by a Beaker) who had been killed with a sharp weapon, though perhaps only in a fight and not a battle. Now the successful warrior wins not only wealth in cattle but also prestige and authority.

But neither wealth nor prowess alone can earn enduring political authority; it must be consecrated. Following the speculations of Durkheim I have already suggested how this consecration might be effected by an individual absorbing the soul-substance of the clan. On his death his tomb would become the shrine where this concentrated soul-substance was conserved. In

---

[1] *Proc.*, lxi, 42.

that case the monuments that suggest the existence of chieftainship would also be testimonies to its consecration. They are, on
the one hand, the great cairns covering richly furnished graves as
at Linlathen (177) and Collessie (200), and on the other the Recumbent Stone cricles of Aberdeenshire (Plate VI, 1). The latter
embody typologically the last version of the architectural tradition
whose initial expression should be the passage-grave of Clava
type, though now the central cairn does not even cover a closed
chamber, as in the later Clava cairns, but merely the pit grave
over which the defunct had been cremated. Whether the defunct
were a Beaker chief is admittedly doubtful—the evidence I
adduced from Old Keig that the primary interment was associated
with flat-rimmed pottery appropriate to stage VIa has not been
refuted by Kilbride-Jones' observations at Loanhead. Even if he
were, the rite of cremation would be more appropriate to stage IV
than III. It is still significant that the conversion of the original
clan vault into a chieftain's tomb and the final result are most
evident in regions exposed, on the testimony of flat axe and
halberd distributions, to penetration by the Irish metal trade.
This observation would support the theoretical arguments
adduced above for a connexion between chieftainship and trade
in metals.

Be that as it may, such evidence as does exist for chiefs belongs
substantially to stage IV. I have already explained why Beaker
No. 77 from the chieftain's cairn at Linlathen and the dagger
from that at Collessie could just as well be attributed to that stage.
The other metal objects found with Beakers too would be more
at home with Food Vessels. Stage III is, in fact, a transitional
epoch. In it we have detected tendencies, but they come to
fruition only in stage IV.

CHAPTER IV

THE HEROIC AGE

BY then, stage IV, the relative increase in the number of graves—if we transfer half the Beaker burials in north-east Scotland from III to IV so as to make the ratio there more nearly equal to what it is in other natural regions, the increase will be from 195 to 355—must denote an expansion of population. This would be accounted for mainly by natural increase but also by the emergence of residual groups—some Megalith-builders in Arran and Kintyre for instance—that had remained outside Beaker society in stage III. There is no need to postulate any substantial immigration of new people, whether from England or Ireland, since the Food Vessel can be explained as a blend of Beaker traditions in potting with those of Neolithic groups—Beacharra and especially Peterborough.

No doubt the surprisingly close analogies of some Scottish Food Vessels (notably Nos. 117, 125, 126 (Plate VII, 1), 282, and 286, from the west and 35 from the north-east) can best be understood if these were made by settlers from Ireland. For among barbarian societies hand-made pots are generally manufactured by women so that an Hibernian style of pottery in Scotland should mean at least an Irishwoman in the Scottish group. But of course such might arrive as a result of intermarriage between families as well as of immigration of families. Moreover the Irish analogies[1] to No. 117 (Plate VII, 3) look like a Scottish fashion and therefore a female Scottish potter from Scotland in Ireland.

Thus any infiltration from Ireland might have been fully offset by the emigration thither of Scottish families or wives. In stage IV, that cultural community between south-western Scotland and northern Ireland that had subsisted in stage II but had been partially interrupted by the Beaker invasion, was fully reconstituted and that in a way that implies interchange of persons by intermarriage or migration of individual families. For the rest the increased population was accommodated only to a minor degree by an extension of the area of settlement; Food Vessel graves spread up the Tay even into Glenlyon and up Eddleston and Leader Waters farther than do Beaker burials (Fig. 10).

[1] *P.P.S.*, iii, 35.

The small cemeteries may imply a rather more sedentary way of life than is demonstrable for stage III. But there is no indication of any radical change in the primary productive economy. Indeed, documents illustrative of this on the Scottish mainland are rarer than before, no domestic sites having been recognized. But if the equations between the mainland and the northern isles set out in Table II be accepted, we may draw on the graphic account of life at Jarlshof, presented by A. O. Curle, giving of course due weight to the peculiarities of the Shetland environment. Admitting that the earlier courtyard houses at Jarlshof are partly synchronous with cist burials of group B and that the latter are systadial with Food Vessel graves, the houses and their original contents would be illustrative of the economy and domestic architecture of stage IV. They give a picture almost as complete as that derived from Skara Brae.

As there, stock-breeding provided one main source of food, and again sheep bones are the commonest in the food-refuse and next bones of cattle. But there are a few pig bones too. Though not numerous, Miss Platt[1] believes they must belong to domestic swine. So pig-breeding, on a restricted scale, had been added to the Bronze Age economy, and pork occasionally varied the Shetlanders' diet. Moreover the pony, too, is represented, albeit sparsely. As the bones are not split for marrow or otherwise butchered, the animal was not used for food.[2] Hence he was not game, but must have been tamed and kept, presumably as a pack animal.

Curle's[3] acute observation revealed a most important advance in rural economy. The rear end of each courtyard house is occupied by a wide deep bay or alcove which in dwelling V, he proved, was used as a cattle-stall. The paved floor was dished to direct the flow of some liquid towards the court (Plate IX, 1). There had stood a tank to receive urine from animals stabled in the alcove and probably a manure heap—the excavator insists on the black and greasy character of the filling here. The alcove or stall, as we may call it, was 10 feet wide (measured at right angles to the axis of the dwelling) and 6½ feet deep. In the side wall of the dwelling was a ring ingeniously contrived from a whale's vertebra to which a tether could be attached so that the beast stood with his hindquarters over the dished area.

The discovery is of twofold significance. Firstly, it is the earliest recorded instance of the stabling of cattle in Britain. Of

[1] *Proc.*, lxvii, 134.   [2] ibid., 133.   [3] *Proc.*, lxix, 89–90.

FIG. 10. DISTRIBUTION OF BURIALS WITH FOOD VESSELS

course the device may have been forced on the Shetlanders by
the exceptionally severe climate and have been peculiar to the
northern isles. But it was practised by lake-dwellers in Switzerland in the Neolithic stage[1] and therefore should not have been
beyond the wit of Bronze Age Britons in general. The practice
not only constituted an advance in animal husbandry but also
provided the cultivator with farmyard manure that seems here
to have been collected with appropriate solicitude. Secondly, it
confirms our *a priori* deduction that herds were individually owned
in as much as the beasts were stalled in individual family dwellings.

In addition to veal, mutton, and pork, the Shetlanders, like the
systadial makers of Food Vessels, depended upon cereal foods.
Querns were found in abundance at Jarlshof; they are in the form
of a trough, open at one end, while the rubbers are generally
broad ovals that could best be pushed with both hands. The
milling was naturally done within the individual dwellings, the
mills being private, i.e. family property; Curle[2] found one in
position near the door in dwelling V.

Finally hunting, fowling, fishing, and collecting supplemented
the results of more active food-production. The bones of seal,
walrus, stork, swan, goose, shag, heron, gannet, and other marine
birds, cod, ling, wrasse, and similar fish, and shells of limpets and
cockles were untidily scattered over the house floors and in the
refuse dumps between dwellings.

The courtyard houses of Jarlshof are elliptical in plan (Fig. 11).
The 'court' is the central area, generally measuring some 10 feet
by 9, which is paved and contains the central hearth, rectangular
and kerbed as at Skara Brae; Curle believes that it was open to
the sky, but as the walls stand only 3 or 4 feet high this cannot be
proved. The stable at the rear was certainly roofed and so were
two smaller cells or alcoves on each side of the court. The functions of these lateral chambers cannot be determined. Beasts and
humans lived under the same roof with only a low partition
between them in the Hebrides last century, but there you padded
through the byre to reach the combined living and sleeping room.
At Jarlshof the livestock would have to pass through the human
habitation. The healthy odour of manure would be equally
pervasive in both cases.

Such an habitation would accommodate only a single family
or at most an enlarged family comprising two generations—
parents and married sons. The several dwellings were not joined

[1] Keller, *Lake Dwellings*, 50.   [2] *Proc.*, lxix, 90.

up into any larger closely unified complex as at Skara Brae and
Rinyo. Indeed we do not know how many dwellings subsisted at
any one time—probably at least three but not more than five.
The whole settlement, whatever its size, was enclosed by a light
wall indistinguishable from a modern dry stone dike and pierced

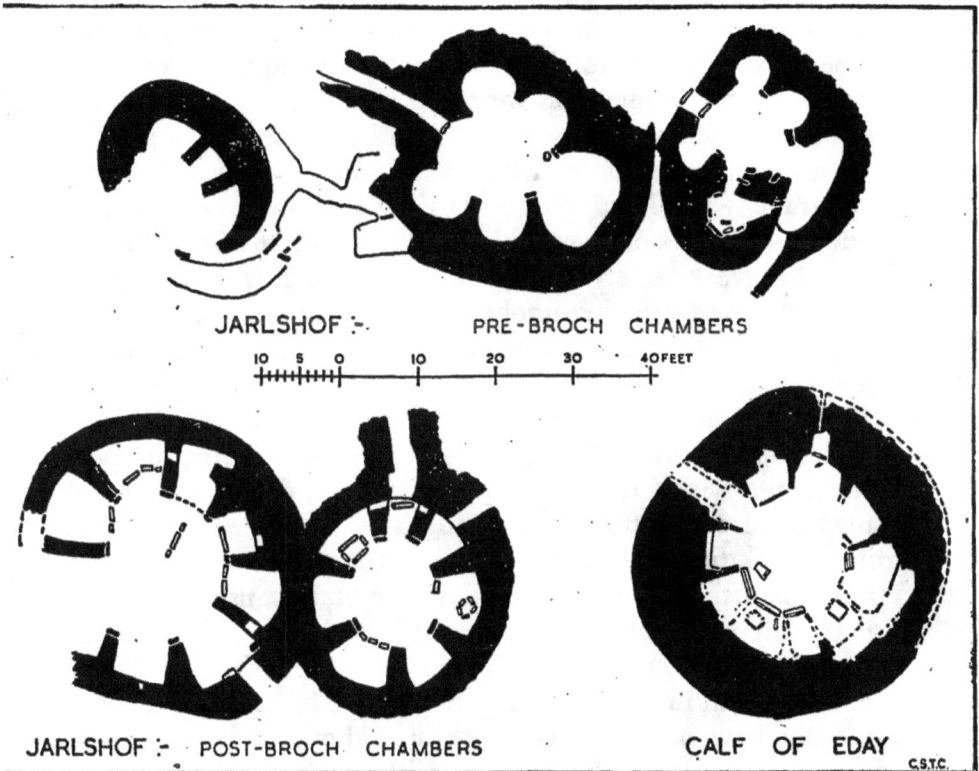

FIG. 11. PLANS OF COURTYARD (TOP) AND WHEEL-HOUSES AFTER CALDER

by a low aperture precisely like the sheep gates left in such dikes
to-day.

Courtyard houses of the Bronze Age have been found only in
Shetland. But in plan a chambered tomb of Quoyness type is so
like a courtyard house converted to sepulchral use and covered
by a narrow roof that they were very likely current in Orkney too.
If translations of the same idea into wood or turf were erected on
the British mainland, they have not survived, but we do find
courtyard houses in Cornwall before the beginning of our era
and in Wales soon after. In any case the small cemeteries of
Food Vessel graves would accommodate the deaths from a
community such as lived round Jarlshof, a unit no larger than

the patriarchal 'great family' or *zadruga*, such as subsisted quite recently among the southern Slavs.

While bronze was quite extensively used outside the northern and western isles by stage IV, its technological importance as a productive force must not be over-estimated. It was probably too costly for industrial use and still employed chiefly for weapons and ornaments. The hoards, no more than the graves, contain no specialized tools beyond flat axes and these might have served as weapons too. Stone tools were still used and manufactured on the Scottish mainland as well as in the isles. In Argyll, a polished stone axe, a fine example of the 'Neolithic celt', was found even in a grave with Food Vessel 117. Contemporary cists have yielded flint knives of several kinds. The Jarlshof villagers manu-factured a great variety of ingenious and specialized implements out of quartz (flint being unobtainable locally), slate, and bone. Many are peculiar to Shetland, but some shapes recur in Orkney too.

Wood was perhaps more skilfully worked than heretofore. In Argyll, round Crinan, the side slabs of cists are provided with grooves into which the end slabs could fit, a device presumably copied from carpentry. A wooden cist thus made of slabs split from an oak tree was actually found in Aberdeenshire and con-tained an urn now lost.[1] Wood was certainly used for vessels side by side with pottery; some Food Vessels are quite obviously copies of wooden bowls (Plate VII, 1) and the false-relief decora-tion thereon an imitation of chip-carving. This mastery of wood-work may have been achieved with the aid of metal tools, but the carvings executed by Polynesians with sharks' teeth and stone show that this assumption is unnecessary. In Orkney and Shet-land, steatite took the place of wood. The manufacture of steatite bowls (Plate VII, 4) would seem to have been a household job like pot-making. In dwelling V at Jarlshof, Curle[2] found three little bowls that appeared to have but newly left the maker's hands and were free from any signs of use, left standing as if to dry. Of course the soft stone could quite easily be carved with quartz implements.

What really distinguishes the economy of stage IV is trade—especially the metal trade—with all its sociological implications. The objects of trade are now varied, numerous, and widely distributed. Jet (really lignite) reached points in Moray, north-east Scotland and Argyll, far away from the natural deposits, in considerable quantities and even Orkney occasionally. The popular ornaments like disc- and spindle-shaped beads and conical buttons with V-perforations may often have been made locally for use. The handsome crescentic necklaces (Plate VIII, 1), the plates of which are richly decorated with rectilinear patterns of finely drilled punctuations look, however, rather like the products of a small school of specialists manufacturing them as commodities for sale. It was surely in this guise that such a necklace—or at least one plate from it—reached Orkney.[1]

Shetland steatite or urns made therefrom must already have been exported in considerable quantities at least to Orkney since steatite urns are found in so many graves there. Certain specialized types of stone implement may also have been objects of trade from or with the northern isles. Mr. Gibson[2] has recently studied the distribution of a particular form of cushion macehead, distributed widely in Great Britain, most specimens of which agree in dimensions to a couple of millimeters. Stray specimens from Fife and from the Hebrides appear to be made of the same sort of rock, believed to occur in nature only in Shetland.

Gold was another important article of trade, albeit only of luxury trade. The metal could be won in the Tay, the Helmsdale, and other rivers. But most of the gold objects found in Scotland in this stage— lunulae, ribbon torques, basket ear-rings—

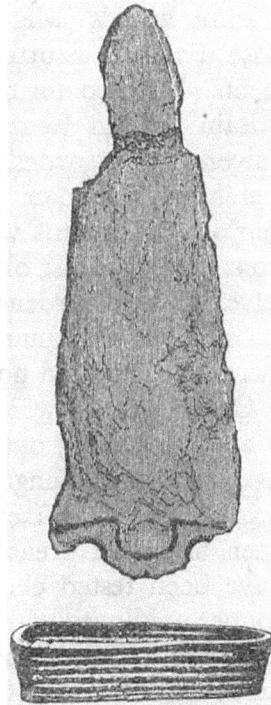

FIG. 12.
ROUND HEELED DAGGER (6 INS. LONG) AND GOLD POMMEL MOUNT, COLLESSIE

are types represented by a far larger number of specimens from Ireland. Even the gold pommel mounts from Camus Cross, Skateraw, and Blackwater Foot, as well as Collessie (Fig. 12) can be paralleled in Ireland. So it looks as if most of our ornaments had been made of Irish gold and imported ready-made from Ireland. Only the gold discs from the Knowes of Trotty (Orkney) have no absolutely exact analogies there or anywhere else.

But the bronze trade occupied a pre-eminent position historically; for bronze was no mere luxury but was becoming a necessity

---

[1] *P.O.A.S.*, xiii, 41.   [2] *Proc.*, lxxviii, 16.

albeit as yet only for defence and offence. As before, the material
and probably the personnel were drawn for the most part from
Ireland. The occurrence of a Food Vessel near Kishorn, where
copper has been mined in recent times and the numbers round
Kilmartin where there is another old copper mine, are at most
ambiguous hints at a possible exploitation of some Scottish lodes
too. Hoards give clues as to the organization of the trade and
the routes taken by the traders.

Some hoards (Migdale, Auchnacree, and the Maidens)[1] com-
prise a mixed assortment of flat axes, knife-daggers, and ornaments. Such conform to the type most commonly found all over
Britain and in Central Europe in the same stage. They are
universally regarded as the stock-in-trade of an itinerant
merchant-craftsman or tinker; such would cater for a local
market; the hoards would have been buried when some danger
from man or beast obliged the wanderers to disembarrass themselves of their burdens by hiding them. The survival of the stock
for modern antiquaries to find indicates the sad fate of the
merchant who had no chance to recover his wares.

Other hoards, which owe their recovery to a like mischance,
consist exclusively of halberds (Baile nan Coile, Auchengoul, New
Machar, and Kingarth), weapons brought almost certainly
ready-made from Ireland, where almost identical weapons have
been found in great numbers; all the Scottish specimens that
have been tested chemically[2] are made, like the Irish ones, of
copper unalloyed with tin. ORiordain[3] suggests that these hoards
illustrate mainly transit trade; their contents would be destined
for re-exportation to Scandinavia. He points out that in Scotland
halberds whether stray or in hoards lie along natural routes
across the country to the North Sea coasts, across Sutherland or
up the Great Glen to the Moray coasts and thence to a likely port
near the Don-Dee estuaries or through the Midland valley to the
Firth of Tay. Thence the adventurous wares would have been
transported by sea again to Jutland and the Elbe ports. Irish
halberds have, in fact, turned up in Denmark and north Germany. Nevertheless there was a local market for halberds here;
in fact as many halberds have been found in graves in Scotland
as in Ireland. So not all the Irish weapons brought here need
have been destined for re-export.

But this transit trade was doubtless very valuable to Food
Vessel societies. In Denmark, southern Sweden, and north

[1] *Proc.*, lvii, 127.   [2] *Proc.*, lxxv, 207, 209.   [3] *Arch.*, lxxxvi, 276.

Germany, very numerous graves quite richly furnished (even though only with a Neolithic equipment in the first two areas) bespeak a large and prosperous population that would offer to adventurous merchants a more enticing and profitable market than the sparse communities wresting a bare livelihood from barren moors and clearings in the Caledonian forests. Moreover the amber of Jutland was a material in universal demand in Bronze Age Europe, to which Scotland had no counterpart to offer; beads of this precious substance have been found in three Scottish graves assignable to stage IV—with Beaker 64, with Food Vessel 42, and forming part of a simple jet necklace under a tumulus in Lanarkshire.[1] Scotland was effectually caught up in the web of international trade in stage IV and apparently owed most of its wealth in metal, such as it was, thereto.

Later on, political events diverted trade with the Baltic and Central Europe to other routes across England. That must be why developed products of the Middle Bronze Age metal work— flanged axes and early palstavs, rapiers, Arreton Down and derivative spear-heads—practically failed to reach Scotland at all and are never found north of the Tay. Only towards the end of stage IV may the 'gold Food Vessel' from Gönnebek, in Holstein, indicate a resumption of the former traffic. It was not till stage V that new types of tools and weapons were disseminated here in any quantity, and at the same time indications of contact with Northern Europe reappear in the archaeological record.

Trade in material goods goes hand in hand with the circulation of ideas. In stage IV, Scotland was again exposed to diffusion. The contribution of Ireland is clear enough. To it we may, for instance, attribute the cup-and-ring markings, those mysterious symbols carved on many rock surfaces particularly in Galloway and round the Firth of Clyde and also on the covers of Food Vessel graves (Plate XIII, 2).

Nevertheless, in intercourse with Ireland, Scotland certainly did not play a merely passive role. For instance, Craw[2] has suggested that the Irish gold lunula is modelled on the Scottish crescentic jet necklace (Plate VIII); both are crescent-shaped collars; the horns of the lunula are divided into panels by engraved lines recalling the spacer-plate necklaces as the incised patterns filling the panels resemble the punctuated patterns adorning the jet spacers. In any case the comparison shows the adoption on both sides of the North Channel of the same fashion—a crescentic

---

[1] *Proc.*, xvi, 149; cf. 1, 57.   [2] *Proc.*, lxiii, 166 ff.

collar—but its translation by preference on each side into the material most easily available locally—jet in Scotland and gold in Ireland. Which reminds us again that in stage IV, as in stage II, a single society occupied both sides of the North Channel, united not indeed by formal political bonds but by commerce, rights of intermarriage, ties of kinship, and consequent communities of fashion and belief.

Trade of the kind now attested must have begun to modify barbarian notions of property. • In all stages, articles used by an individual were presumably accepted as his personal possessions —extensions of his person in fact. But the bronzes in a merchant's hoard were not designed for his personal use, but for sale. They were commodities as well as possessions. Soon they might become wealth and the accumulation of commodities an end in itself in so far as their possession was not only a convenience and a source of private gratification, but conferred also social prestige and came to symbolize rank.

Now the costly commodities purveyed by the bronze-worker could confer power. The halberds and the stout daggers like those from Gilchorn, Westermains of Auchterhouse, and Blackwater Foot (Fig. 13) were very effective weapons. But, owing to their high social cost, they were evidently the monopoly of a few. The tombs containing the weapons just mentioned are marked out by the size of the cist or of the covering cairn as the graves of chiefs. The monopoly of such effective weapons must have raised their possessors above challenge and reinforced their authority as did the knight's costly armour in the Middle Ages. The representation of flat axes on the walls of two large cist graves near Kilmartin (Plate XIII, 2) emphasizes the value attached to such costly weapons and may mean they had a magical potency too. No wonder, then, the factors mentioned on p. 48, being thus intensified and supplemented, that we find abundant sepulchral evidence for chieftainship by stage IV.

The cist burials with Food Vessels at the centres of circles of great stones (12, 144-5, 190) must certainly rank as graves of chiefs or chieftainesses and so probably should the cremations in the Recumbent Stone circles of the north-east, if they are correctly referred to stage IV. The same must be said of the extended burials in long cists. In Egypt, Greece, Sicily, and Central Europe, the change from contracted to extended burial was a concomitant of increasing wealth quite without ethnic significance;[1]

[1] *Man*, 1945, No. 4.

in Egypt, for instance, it began as the prerogative of Pharaoh and his nobles about 3000 B.C. and gradually spread down the social ladder till by 2000 only the very poorest were still buried doubled up.[1] In Scotland the process was presumably arrested by the spread of cremation.

The richly furnished graves under huge cairns, like the dagger graves just mentioned or the largest of the Knowes of Trotty with its gold discs and amber beads belong no less certainly to chiefs. The double cist at Auchterhouse may, indeed, be an example of the immolation of the wife at her husband's funeral, a practice that, like human sacrifice, is more often associated with the obsequies of chiefs than of private persons. But unfortunately the cremation of both bodies and the absence of distinctive furniture with one precluded the determination of the sex in this instance. At Duncracaig, too, the central cist contained a cremated and an unburned body while a third skeleton lay on the capstone.

Apart from these instances attested by rich grave goods, I expect that the majority of

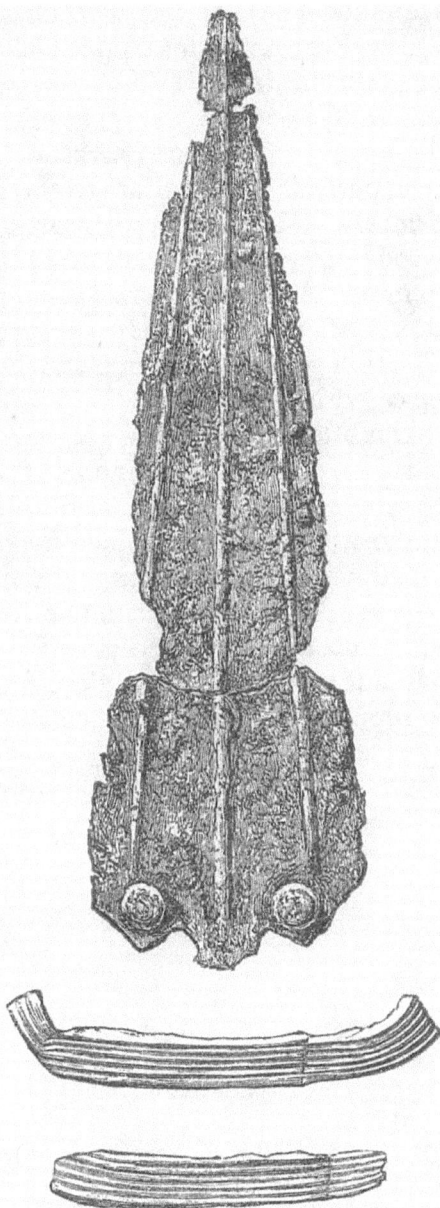

FIG. 13. MID-RIB DAGGER WITH GOLD POMMEL MOUNT, BLACKWATER FOOT, ARRAN. $\frac{1}{2}$

our larger hill-top cairns are tombs of chiefs of stage IV. In some of these great cairns where the central cist had been robbed, secondary cists appropriate to stage IV (Hatton Cairn, Angus;

[1] Petrie, Brunton, etc., *Qau and Badari*, i, 51.

Harelaw, Fife), or intrusive cinerary urns of V (Queen Mary's Cairn, East Kilbride; Upper Dallachy, Banffs.), would assign the primary burial to IV. A few apparently intact have yielded miserably poor relics. The Stroanfreggan Cairn,[1] 86 feet in diameter, in Glenkens (Kirkcud.), contained only a slug knife—a relic perfectly appropriate to the Food Vessel complex but hardly princely. Of course, in such cases, the possibility of quite valuable wooden grave goods, now completely vanished, should be borne in mind. As already noted, some clay Food Vessels are manifestly copies of, perhaps cheap substitutes for, carved wooden bowls. The thin gold vessel from Gönnebek suggests that such might even be cased in gold.

Doubtless the chiefs, interred beneath such monumental barrows, were still felt, and felt themselves, as representatives and trustees of the clans, endowed indeed with spiritual and temporal authority, but still restrained by kinship bonds. So far had metal instruments of production and the commodities so produced gone by stage IV to relax 'primitive communism'. But just so far had that relaxation been necessary for their circulation and use. They had not yet released really productive forces nor created supplies to support new productive classes.

[1] *Proc.*, xlv, 432.

CHAPTER **V**

THE LATE BRONZE AGE

NO less than 665 interments are assigned to stage V, more than
double the number attributable to stage IV. Such an increase
in graves must denote a quite substantial expansion of population especially as hardly any graves of this stage are recorded
from the West Highlands where presumably type A Food
Vessels took the place of Overhanging Rim Urns. Now, while
isolated burials occur in Cinerary Urns as with Beakers and Food
Vessels, a good two-thirds—at least 405—come from urnfield
cemeteries; in Fife the proportion rises as high as 138 out of 168.
The numbers of burials reported from such cemeteries range from
5 to 31. These figures, particularly the lower ones, are undoubtedly too low; most urnfields have been exposed in the
course of agricultural or commercial operations and not systematically or exhaustively searched by experts so that some urns and
many unurned cremations have remained unnoted; at Loanhead,[1]
the only urnfield deliberately excavated, 19 out of 31 cremations
lay in the bare earth. But though the recorded figures must be
augmented by an incalculable amount, the size of the communities
denoted by the urnfields must not be over-estimated.

In each such cemetery more than one stage in the degeneration
of the Overhanging Rim Urn (Fig. 14) is represented, as the
following table shows.

Overhanging Rim	Stage	II	III	IV-V	Encrusted	Enlarged Food Vessel
Loanhead of Daviot[1] (77–107)	I	2	3	0		5
Brackmont Mill[2] (191–209)	6	4	0	0		0
St. Andrews[3] (274–293)	0	?12	?10	1		?
Calais Moor[4] (311–320)	I	1	4			
Magdalen Bdg.[5] (408–435)	?	2	5			
Kirk Park[6] (436–460)		4	2			

Of course we do not know how long this regular degenerative
process took, nor can we assert that it proceeded everywhere at
a uniform rate. But three generations would surely be an extreme
minimum. Moreover, cremation and inurnment were by no

[1] *Proc.*, lxx, 278. [2] lxxi, 256; lxxvi, 84. [3] xli, 412. [4] xx, 246. [5] xvi, 419. [6] xxviii, 65.

means confined to adults; at Brackmont Mill 3 out of 11 cremations were of 'infants or very young children', while 8 out of 31
at Loanhead were of children between three and six. On the
basis of calculation used by Rademacher 35 graves would be
required by a community of 21 persons in 120 years (Der Volk-
stamm zwischen Sieg-Wupper-Rhein zur ersten Eisenzeit, *Mann.
Erg. Bd.*, 5, 1927; being based on a Rhenish village of the nine-
teenth century, his mortality rate is too small for a Bronze Age
community).

Such a cemetery would then accommodate the fatalities in a
single patriarchal clan or great-household of the zadruga type.
The arrangements of the cemeteries too would be appropriate to
a social unit of this kind and size. At Loanhead of Daviot
(Plate X, 1) all the burials were grouped within a circular
enclosure 35 ft. in diameter with a cremation *in situ* at the centre.
At Dalnavie (6–21)[1] fifteen inverted urns stood around a larger
central one in a space 54 ft. across bounded by 'a low circular
turf fence'. Arrangements of urns in a circle have been reported
also in Fife and Nithsdale, as well as in northern England. The
central grave contained the remains of an important person. At
Dalnavie the central urn is explicitly stated to have been twice
as large as the rest and to have been accompanied by a 'stone
axe'—presumably a battle-axe. At Loanhead the central grave-
pit contained the ashes of an adult male who had been laid upon
the pyre in the old contracted attitude and cremated on the spot.
As this cemetery, judging by the wide typological variation of
the urns, includes the remains of several generations, the group
can hardly represent a chief surrounded by his retainers; for in
each generation the chief's successors should occupy the centre
of a new group. The same argument would doubtless apply to
other cases where the urns have been lost or the central grave
not observed. The central burial is rather that of the patriarch,
the founder of the community, whose children and grandchildren
were buried in the enclosure first sanctified by his obsequies.

A Scottish urnfield cannot, therefore, be regarded as the
counterpart of the Late Bronze Age urnfields of southern England
which, containing as many as a hundred interments, must correspond to a small village. It corresponds rather to the same sort
of settlement as a Food Vessel cemetery—a lone steading (if such
a term do not imply an unwarranted degree of fixity) rather than
a village, perhaps the sort of unit that could later occupy one

[1] *T.G.S.I.*, 1886, 64.

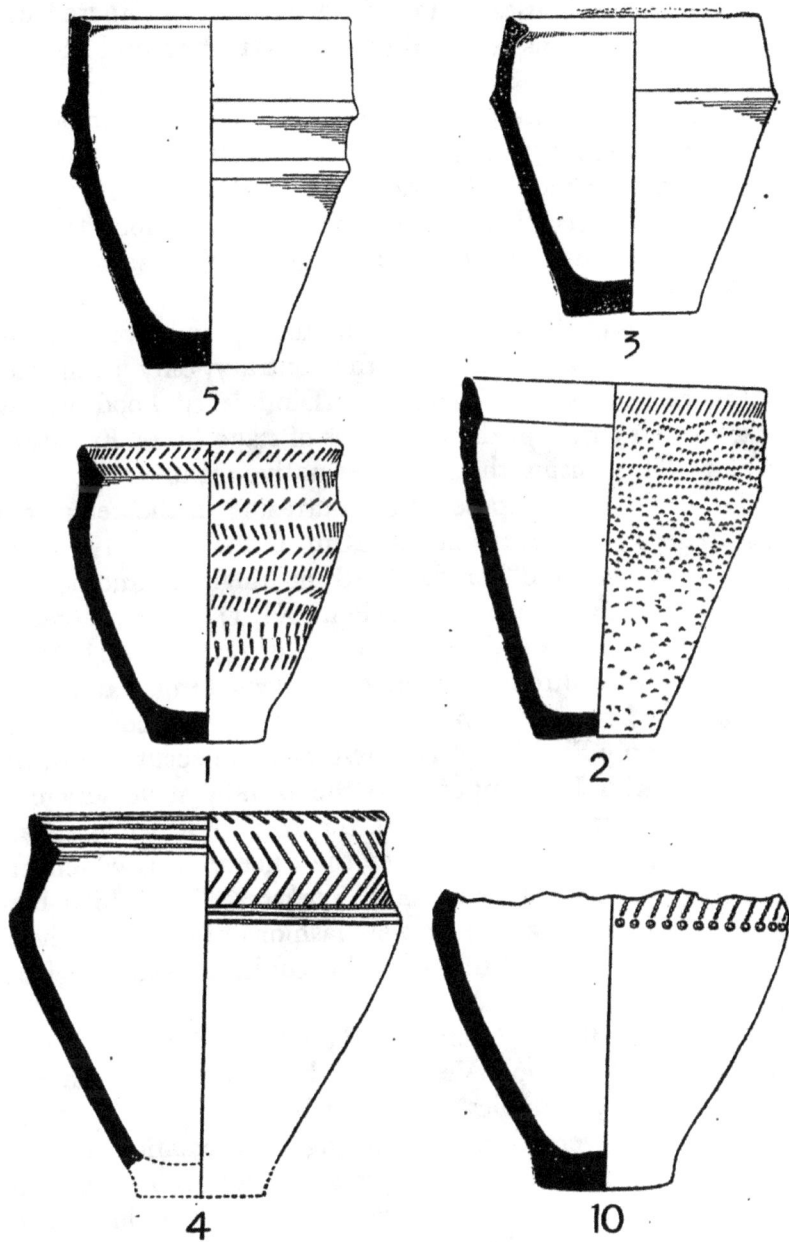

FIG. 14. CORDONED (5), BICONICAL (3), AND ENLARGED FOOD VESSEL
URNS, LOANHEAD OF DAVIOT, ½

of the great round houses—larger in area than our sacred en-
closures—that Bersu has revealed to us in Wiltshire and the Isle
of Man.

The growth of population in stage V is, however, indicated
not only by the enlargement of the local units above what we
knew in IV, but by the relative density of such units. To realize
this it is enough to recall the large urnfields that happen to have
been noted between Leith and Musselburgh or those on either
side of the Eden estuary.

The expansion of the unit and of the total population was not
due solely to natural increase. On the contrary, only a minority
of the funerary urns are Enlarged or Diminished Food Vessels
(Fig. 14, 1) that carry on the traditions of stage IV or Encrusted
Urns (Plate XI, 2) using the still older native technique of Skara
Brae. To these are juxtaposed and contrasted in the cemeteries
a large majority of Overhanging Rim Urns. This type was
apparently created and standardized in England and spread
northward only in an evolved form (Plate XI, 1). As it suffered in
time a regular typological degeneration (Fig. 14, 5, 3), its gradual
progress northward through Scotland is reflected in the diminish-
ing proportion of early forms from our northern counties till
beyond the Beauly Firth only the latest varieties occur. With the
Overhanging Rim Urn appear too the equally novel usage of
accessory Pigmy Vessels (Plate X, 2), the forms of which again are
generally English, stone battle-axes the ancestors of which are
again discoverable in Wiltshire and Yorkshire, but which here
develop fresh features, and even new fashions of dress—an ivory
buckle from Brackmont Mill faithfully copies a gold one from
Wiltshire.[1]

However much the Overhanging Rim Urn itself may owe to
the Beaker and the Food Vessel and however freely the new
fashion in funerary ceramics may have been adopted by native
societies here that were already favouring the cremationist ritual,
the new type of ossuary in its mature form and accompanied by
the other innovations enumerated can only have been introduced
and spread by an actual infiltration of urn-folk from beyond the
Cheviots. But their advent must not be taken to denote a replacement of population or even a conquest. Diminished and Enlarged
Food Vessels are proof enough of the survival of the old population
and their vigour in stage V. Their occurrence side by side with
Overhanging Rim Urns in urnfields that represent the consecrated

[1] *Proc.*, lxxv, 205; lxxvi, 91.

LEWIS
SKYE
MORAY FIRTH
MOUNTH
R TAY
FIRTH OF FORTH
TWEED
ARRAN
FIRTH OF CLYDE
GALLOWAY
Cinerary Urn
Urn Field

FIG. 15. DISTRIBUTION OF CREMATION BURIALS IN CINERARY URNS

burial-grounds of the clans indicates the complete and equal union of the groups. In fact a backwash of northern families may be inferred from the spread of Encrusted Urns into northern England and Wales.

How then was the enlarged population supported? Stage V, being equivalent to the Late Bronze Age of typologists, certainly saw a release of new productive forces.

Metal first became relatively abundant and consequently cheap —cheap enough to be applied effectively to productive uses— during stage V. The reduction in the cost of bronze is the outstanding characteristic of the Late Bronze Age, not only in Scotland but throughout Europe and far into Asia. It can be deduced not so much from the increase in the absolute number of relics—in Scotland, for example, we have 250 socketed celts of known provenance as against 140 flat celts —but from the nature of the relics. For now bronze was used not only for weapons and ornaments, but for common utensils—knives and razors—for craftsmen's tools—adzes, gouges, chisels, light hammers (Plate XII, 1) and small anvils (Fig. 16)— even agricultural implements like sickles (Fig. 17); the weapons themselves are larger and heavier—swords up to 24 inches long and formidable spearheads; very large objects—buckets, cauldrons, and shields—were hammered out of bronze. Such metal equipment signalized a distinct advance in society's productive forces and control over the environment.

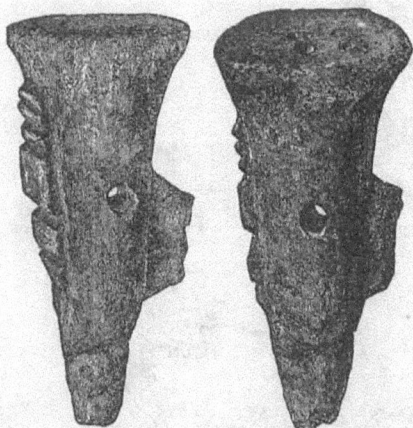

FIG. 16. METAL WORKER'S ANVIL OF BRONZE, 4 INS. LONG, KYLE OF OYKEL, SUTHERLAND

The revolution was not, as a whole, the result of any processes discovered, or economic reforms initiated, in Scotland or indeed the British Isles; precisely the same phenomena characterize this stage from the Atlantic to the Jenissei, from Sicily to Denmark. They are on the available evidence manifested rather earlier in Central Europe than in Britain, and definitely earlier in southern England than in Scotland—a detailed study of swords and axes, for instance, reveals three typological phases of which only the latest is clearly represented here. The metallurgical revolution is the result of historical events mostly enacted outside our narrow stage.

Their nature is not fully understood, but certain moments can be recognized.[1] In the Austrian Alps the exploitation of deep-seated copper lodes and the smelting of unoxidized sulphide ores after a preliminary roasting are first attested in the Late Bronze Age; previously surface deposits that can never have been very rich, but could be smelted without preliminary treatment, probably supplied all the copper used in Europe this side of the Alps. But neither monumental evidence for the new technique

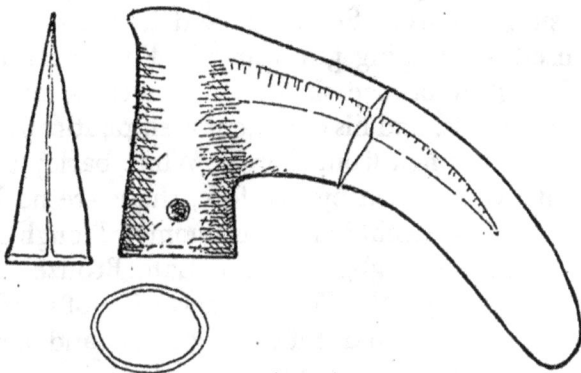

FIG. 17. SOCKETED SICKLE OF BRONZE, DORES, INVERNESS. ½
AFTER FOX

of mining in hard rock nor yet chemical evidence for the employment of sulphide ores has yet been reported in the British Isles.

'Founders' hoards' consisting largely of scrap metal—old and battered weapons and tools—are distinctive of the Late Bronze Age from the Severn to the Dnieper. They must denote a re-organization of the distributive branch of the industry to ensure a scrupulous collection of salvage. Only one Scottish hoard, that from Duddingston Loch,[2] is typical of this class, but those from Islay[3] and Ballymore, Cowal,[4] might be classed here, though unusually small.

A new technique of casting may be deduced from fragmentary clay moulds found on Traprain Law, at Loanhead of Daviot, and at Jarlshof, as well as in Yorkshire and northern Ireland. This innovation is not attested for the earlier part of the Late Bronze Age—as we know it in England—and may therefore be an invention of Highland Britain in general if not Scotland in

---

[1] *J.R.A.I.*, xliv (1944), 11.   [2] *Proc.*, lvi, 360.   [3] ibid., xvi, 409.
[4] ibid., lxxvii, 184.

particular. The other innovations must have percolated to us by 'diffusion'.

Within the existing relations of production the benefits conferred by cheaper bronze were not very startling and confined to a limited circle. In the domain of primary production fresh lands might be opened to cultivation by a freer use of metal axes. Cinerary Urns marked in notoriously forested regions that were blank on earlier maps in Annandale and lower Nithsdale and less conspicuously in the Ayrshire valleys thus indicate penetration where oak woods had formerly been a bar to settlement. Bronze sickles might have helped the farmer to reap his crop. But only three have survived from Scotland, and it is doubtful whether they were used for reaping grain at all. Fox[1] remarks that the majority of English bronze sickles do not come from the best corn-growing regions, and his comment is emphatically applicable to the Scottish specimen from Dores. While barley and flax, as well as wheat, were grown by urn-folk, there are no indications of any radical improvement in rural economy. Plough cultivation, initiated in southern England in the Late Bronze Age, is still unattested here in stage V. The concentration of urnfields along the Lothian, Ayrshire, and Fifeshire coasts, and generally on sandy tracts, indicates the same preference for poor light soils, as had been manifested by Beaker and Food Vessel societies. The cemeteries on the Ayrshire moors would be as appropriate to a pastoral régime as were those of stage III. Arrow-heads from five graves may still be taken as indicative of hunting. A local group of the size deduced from the urnfields could in fact be maintained by the economy ruling in stages III and IV.

Specialized metal tools might symbolize the emergence of new specialized craftsmen supported, like bronze-smiths, from the surplus of primary production. But the only craft that might thus be deduced is carpentry. The carpenter's kit was, however, still very restricted as far as metal tools are concerned. To it can probably be reckoned the socketed gouges and just possibly the oddly curved knives, but not the light socketed hammers; metal saws are conspicuously absent from the hoards. It is questionable whether such a restricted range of tools require the assumption of professional carpenters. The only craftsmen whose equipment was really substantially enlarged by cheaper metal tools were the metal-workers themselves. To them undoubtedly belong the hammers and anvils—for embossing and similar fine work only—

[1] *P.P.S.*, v (1939), 239.

while gouges and even the curved knives would come in handy in the preparation of moulds and other operations round the smithy. But even the smith still lacked proper tongs, as throughout the whole Bronze Age world, including even the Ancient East, and in the British Isles heavy hammers of metal were unavailable.

Trade certainly revived and expanded. Political and economic changes in the international field—the expansion of 'Urnfield folk' from Central Europe and the subsequent spread northward and westward of iron-working, perhaps also an incorporation of northern Ireland in the south-west Scottish cultural-province—combined to divert the Irish metal trade towards Scotland as a result of the obstruction of the more southerly routes developed in the Middle Bronze Age (p. 59) and the subsequent curtailment of the demand for bronze in areas where iron was available. After the temporary isolation during Middle Bronze Age 2 and Late Bronze Age 1–2, Scotland was again caught up in the full current of north-west European commerce.

Hoards and stray finds illustrate the re-use of the routes across Scotland defined by halberds and flat axes in the Earlier Bronze Age. Late Bronze Age hoards from Torran near Ford and Monmore, Killin, may indicate the opening-up of a new route from the west coast near Crinan via Loch Awe and Loch Tay to Strathmore and the Firth of Tay. Still more explicitly do the numerous hoards and isolated relics from the Western Isles and Orkney commemorate the circumnavigation of Scotland by frail merchantmen with cargoes destined for the Scandinavian market. These voyages may be only a resumption of 'Stone Age' traffic deduced from the similarities of sepulchral architecture in Denmark, northern and western Scotland (groups B and C), and Ireland. Even so, improvements in boat-building, made possible by cheaper bronze tools, must have contributed to the revival.

Judged by the shapes that recur repeatedly in Ireland most of the Late Bronze Age gold work and bronze work was either made in Ireland or made in imitation of fashionable Irish types. But there is a fair sprinkling of no less distinctive English types. For instance, of the socketed celts 18[1] are typical 'Yorkshire axes', as defined by Fox. As a reflex of continental trade some Central and North European forms figure in Scottish hoards as actual imports like the bronze cup from Adabrock (Plate XII, 1), or as local imitations—sunflower and cup-head pins, bracelets of Covesea type[2] and collars with attached ringlets[3] like those from Wester

---

[1] *Proc.*, lxxii, 154.   [2] ibid., lix, 113.   [3] ibid., lxv, 183.

Ord and Braes of Gight. The amber beads from Adabrock and Balmashanner may safely be regarded as of Baltic origin. Similar beads occur in contemporary Irish hoards.

Bronze was certainly worked in Scotland in stage V, since the moulds and tools of the workers are relatively numerous. The stone moulds for socketed axes, spear-heads, and other Late Bronze Age implements presumably belonged to perambulating smiths and merchant artificers such as had been the chief agents in the production and distribution of metal-ware since stage III. The find-spots mark where they had been lost, not necessarily the site of a smithy where they had been used. The clay moulds mean something quite different. They are not forms in which a whole series of objects have been and will be cast, but fragments of moulds that had been built up on a pattern, used once for a casting, and then broken to obtain the product. Craftsmen did not carry such about with them, but made them and discarded them in the workshop.

The implications of this procedure are revealed by Curle's excavations at Jarlshof. While courtyard house I was still habitable, a bronze-smith reached the southern tip of Shetland and turned the dwelling into his workshop. The excavator found the ashes of the hearth, the casting pit in which the finished mould would be stood in sand while molten metal was run in, a bin of clay from which the moulds were made together with a quern converted into a kneading trough, and innumerable fragments of moulds, jets, and lumps of metal.

The smith had been trained in the Irish school since his products are of explicitly Irish forms. Very likely he arrived with a stock of Irish products to serve as patterns; the clay plug for a knife-socket found at Jarlshof actually fits the socket of a bronze knife from Ireland exactly. But having arrived, the smith settled down; moulds testifying to his activity turned up in buildings belonging to two or three architectural phases. He became, in fact, a resident smith. Presumably he used and smelted local ores—no analyses are available. But he would have to import his tin—if he used any, and presumably also the Scots fir, oak, hazel, and willow charcoal he certainly did use. He manufactured axes, swords, knives, and pins, and that on a fairly generous scale judging by the multitude of mould-fragments. Was he producing primarily for local consumption? Not one of his or any contemporary's products has yet come to light in Shetland outside the hamlet. The alternative is, however, *a priori* unlikely; this remote northern archipelago is an unsuitable location for a factory producing for a British market and none of the types it specialized in was current outside the British Isles. The artisan operating at Jarlshof may have been more than a village smith, but his customers were probably confined to the islanders.

By settling down presumably with his family the perambulating smith may have gained in security. But considering the limitation of his clientele and the smallness of the social surplus likely to be available with the prevailing rural economy, his remuneration cannot have been generous. Indeed the transformation of the itinerant artificer 'welcomed everywhere', as Homer says of the earlier Bronze Age, into a resident smith hardly spelled an advance in the economic status of the craft. One doubts whether it were voluntary. It might have been imposed on the bronze-worker by growing competition of iron—Late Bronze Age 3 in Scotland and Ireland is certainly contemporary with Iron Age A in southern England and the Hallstatt period of the Continent—and the consequent restriction of the market for bronze tools and weapons. In such a crisis the most talented craftsmen in bronze eventually found patrons and esteem in the courts of La Tène war-lords. The rest must sell their meaner skill to the rustics of the Lothians, Aberdeenshire, and Shetland.

How were they fitted into the kinship system? Or were they not admitted save as the slaves of the local clan or clan chief? Was our friend at Jarlshof a captive carried off in a raid on Ireland, such as was to become common in early historical times? The beginnings of such exploitation of labour may well go back to stage V.

In any case trade was essential for the existence of a Bronze Age since the industrial metals had to be imported nearly every-where. Its extent and vigour during stage V is shown by the large number of hoards and scattered metal products and the variety of objects and materials comprised therein. Commodity production and exchange were more vigorous than ever in any previous stage; specialization of labour and trade were intensified. This situation demanded an abstract standard of value—something for which bulls, buckets, and bracelets could alike be exchanged, in a word—Money.

During the Late Bronze Age, albeit only near its end, an approximation to the requisite standard was in fact established by social convention in Scotland and Ireland. The Balmashanner hoard[1]

---

[1] *Proc.*, xxvi, 182.

and contemporary Irish hoards contain thick slug-shaped golden rings that are universally accepted as units of currency—ring money (Plate XII, 2). Others were found in a cave near Covesea (Moray),[1] inhabited first in Stage VIa, and stray. All these unminted Scottish 'coins' consist, not of solid gold, but of bronze overlaid with thin gold foil. Are they base coin foisted upon our unsophisticated ancestors by crafty merchants from Eire or devised by canny Scots to deceive the latter or merely a low denomination suited to the transactions of a poor and frugal society? In any case a 'natural economy' has now been left behind and money transactions are taking the place of direct barter.

This incipient standardization of values symbolizes further a social recognition of a new concept of wealth. By stage V the number, and still more the variety, of things one could own and use or wear had evidently increased enormously. Such must now have been felt as more than mere extensions of their owner's personality as the individually used possessions of stage II had still been. They were at least commodities, things that could be exchanged; they were potentially wealth, things desired for the sake of possession and not for use. They became symbols of prestige, rank, authority, even if they did not actually confer them. Among the most conspicuous items in inventories of stage V are luxury objects of parade—collars, bracelets, and other ornaments of bronze and gold, amber and even glass beads and bronze cups. Even the most useful of the novelties—the metal cauldrons and buckets—must have been scarce and fantastically expensive. They were doubly valuable. They were not only useful in enabling their happy owner for the first time to seethe meat and boil water over the fire instead of by dropping heated but inevitably dirty stones into a pot. But also the possession of such an article conferred prestige and was *de facto* the prerogative of the wealthy few, if not the *de jure* privilege of the highest rank. In the funerary records of the Bronze Age metal cauldrons figure among the grave goods only of the royal tombs of Ur, of the shaft-graves of Mycenae's kings, of some rich Caucasian chieftains' graves, and similar princely sepulchres. In the literature of Heroic Ages cauldrons receive especial mention from Homer among the treasures of Priam and of Achaean kings and similarly among treasures enumerated in the Irish epic poems. Even the Welsh laws and similar documents of a later age still bear witness to the high estimation of these great metal vessels. In fact only six

_____
[1] *Proc.*, lxv, 181.

cauldrons have survived from the Bronze Age of Scotland even in bits as against thirty from Ireland.

None of these come from graves. Of the contemporary ornaments only three gold armlets come from graves. A pair are reported to have been found lying on the capstone of a short cist in the big urnfield at Alloa. The third is described as having been found with Cinerary Urn 48 in an intrusive secondary burial under a cairn at Upper Dallachy, Banffs. As the group is lost, it may belong to stage VI, like a cremation interment accompanied by a gold armlet from Duff House in the same county. None of the other metal tools, weapons, nor ornaments distinctive of stage V has ever been found in a grave.

Indeed, as was remarked earlier, burials of stage V are very poorly furnished with gear. In only some fifty out of 665 have any possessions at all been found buried with the defunct's ashes, and these were for the most part poor flint implements or trinkets of little worth, and that despite the multiplication of commodities. Just the same impoverishment of funerary furniture contrasting with an equal increase of possible possessions is a feature of the Late Bronze Age throughout the British Isles, and indeed in most parts of Europe—particularly in East-central Europe, South Russia, Sicily, and even Denmark. From a survey of burials over a much wider range of space and time I[1] have deduced a general rule, that in a stable society the richness of grave furniture tends to decline though society's wealth increase.

Discussing this phenomenon in the barrows of the South Russian steppes, Kruglov and Podgayetskiĭ[2] bring it into connexion with the new conception of wealth and appropriate adjustments of property relations. In a communistic society a person's possessions being what he used, and wore, and very often made himself, and so truly attributes of his person, were naturally buried or cremated with his body. But now they have become commodities, wealth, sources of prestige and symbols of status. The accumulation of commodities may then become an end in itself, and that not only for the individual, but for that more enduring unit, the family. Now if possessions can be exchanged and so dissociated from their user, they can also be inherited. It was in the family's interest to accumulate gold ornaments, bronze swords, and cauldrons, not to bury them in a grave or consume them on a pyre. To put it bluntly, the greed of the heirs discouraged extravagant funerary furniture. If this convincing

[1] *Man*, 1945, No. 4. [2] *Rodovoe Obshchestvo Stepeĭ Vostochnoĭ Evropy*, Moskva, 1935.

argument be accepted, the depressing poverty of stage V graves affords confirmation for the social acceptance of the conceptions of wealth already indicated.

An appropriate ideology would salve the survivors' consciences. Now it has been argued by Rohde and many others that the replacement of inhumation by cremation signifies a new and less materialistic conception of life after death. The soul would be released from the gross body by the flames and ascend with the smoke in a more ethereal shape. And it would hardly need material swords and bracelets either. If this theory be correct, the new conception it postulates would, of course, excuse a practice commended by more practical considerations. No one, of course, maintains that the doctrine was deliberately invented to justify funereal stinginess. But the economic motive would eventually favour its adoption. In Scotland burial practice suggests that the rite came before the theory—as rites generally do. Cremation was not uncommonly practised in stage IV, and may have begun even in II. And these earlier cremation burials are not especially poorly furnished. But a more spiritualized conception of the soul would be a perfectly logical rationalization of the cremationist rite. And then that rationalization would be welcomed as condoning a practice dictated by purely mundane considerations. In this sense the spread of cremation during stage IV and culminating in V and the parallel reduction of grave goods would be but the consecration of a new conception of property and wealth.

A corollary of the new idea of wealth would be an accentuation of the stratification of society; to the contrast between chief and commoner would be added that between rich and poor. Very likely the members of each contrasted pair would coincide; riches and chieftainship would still go together. The social surplus must still have been diminutive so that only by concentration would enough be available to purchase those forms of wealth that figure most prominently in our lists—imported metal-ware. For despite the reduction of cost, bronze as well as gold must have remained very expensive. The most natural centres of accumulation would be the old chieftainships.

Now it is true that evidences for this rank are less conspicuous in stage V than in IV. I do not know any large cairn certainly erected to cover a primary burial in a Cinerary Urn. While interments of stage V have been reported from several stone circles, none are demonstrably primary. At the same time it might be expected *a priori* that the reduction in the cost of bronze armament would undermine that buttress to the chieftain's power (p. 60). But of course such a tendency would be offset by the introduction of costly defensive arms in the shape of shields that must have been the prerogative of a few like the knight's armour of our Middle Ages.

A few graves do in fact stand out from the general poverty, not indeed for wealth, but by containing ceremonial objects. It would accord with the practice of modern barbarians if these had been sacrificed by the greedy heirs because their ceremonial use by their deceased owner had impregnated them with a dangerous magic. The ornate bronze razors found in ten graves have been correctly diagnosed by Mahr as ritual implements appropriate to the toilet of one performing priestly functions. Two such functionaries were buried in the urnfield at Law Park, St. Andrews. The handsome stone battle-axes or mace-heads (Plate X, 3) that survive from nine other graves must rank as emblems of authority rather than as effective weapons in an age of bronze swords, spears, and shields. The authority they symbolized was obviously military, but it might have been purely personal, even elective, certainly not hereditary, in which case its symbols would naturally have to be buried with its wielder. Even though a small unornamented blade that might have been a razor accompanied the Sandmill battle-axe, the leadership attested by such emblems would seem something different from the sacred chieftainship of stage IV. The latter, of course, would have persisted in the West Highlands if we are correct in assuming that burials with type A Food Vessels are there synchronous, if not systadial, with Cinerary Urns elsewhere.

Whether or no chieftainship survived in stage V and whatever change it had undergone, it would follow from the very nature of the new bronzes, as much from general considerations already advanced, that their acquisition was still confined to a relatively small class within society. Save for the metal-workers' own equipment and some axes used for clearing land the products of the improved and expanded bronze industry of stage V are not instruments of production, but gear for warriors and trappings for their wives. In other words, the reduction in the cost of bronze did not, and under existing relations of production could not, release any very potent new forces for the production of wealth.

At the same time the new conception of wealth must have stimulated acquisitiveness. Now even more easily than the old wealth in cattle could the new desirable commodities be acquired by seizing what others had produced instead of producing them oneself. The novel standards, in other words, provide a fresh inducement to warfare. The superabundance of efficient weapons of war in the metal inventories of stage V justifies the deduction of intensified fighting, more frequent cattle-raids, and plundering expeditions.

By stage V Bronze Age society was involved in a double contradiction: it could neither provide for its growing numbers by radical improvements in food production, nor yet find a regular outlet for the surplus in expanding industry and commerce. The increased output of the metal industry—the only secondary industry adequately reflected in the archaeological record—was diverted to the use of warriors and war-lords. Those who alone were in a position to purchase its products were too few to constitute a flexible effective market for expanding production so that its capacity to absorb more workers was rigidly limited. Indeed, I have already given reasons for thinking that the status of bronze-smiths was declining in stage V.

The impasse could be avoided by a resort to arms. The appearance of Cinerary Urns and battle-axes of Scottish derivation in northern Ireland looks more like a hostile invasion than a friendly interchange of families such as might suffice to explain Hiberno-Caledonian relations in stages II and IV. It may indeed represent a successful attempt to accommodate a population overflowing from Galloway on stolen Irish soil and so indicate a pressure on and competition for the land in Scotland. The invasion may at the same time have had the effect of forcibly diverting to Scotland a share in the produce of the Irish metallurgical industry and trade. I should like to regard the early Glentrool hoard,[1] referrable to Late Bronze Age 1, and contemporary stray bronzes that are found only in Galloway and Ayrshire as indirectly first-fruits of the expedition.

On the other hand, the use of a Food Vessel of the distinctively Hibernian type, E, as an ossuary in the urnfield at Brackmont Mill, would suggest that in the sequel peaceful intercourse between the two islands was re-established and consolidated as in stage IV. The urn must surely have been made by an Hibernian woman, and for a person of Irish extraction who had died as a member of the Fifeshire community in whose burial-ground the ashes were interred.

[1] *Proc.*, lv, 29.

But if the Urn-folk in Scotland found it simpler to conquer land in Ireland for their younger sons with bronze swords than to clear the Caledonian forests with bronze axes, other societies had hit upon the same idea. Armed with plentiful iron weapons, Brythonic Celts from Gaul and southern England turned against Scotland the device our Late Bronze Age inhabitants seem to have applied to Ireland. If the changes in burial practice and ceramic technique that first mark the transition to stage VI may conceivably be explained as results of internal development, the outstanding monuments of the stage, the Gallic forts and the brochs, were almost certainly erected by fresh invaders. But these brought blacksmiths in their train and a partial solution for the first contradiction.

ADDENDUM: PREHISTORIC AGRICULTURE

The Megalith-builders cultivated barley—in Orkney already bere—in stage II. Imprints of barley-grains, but none of wheat, have been identified on sherds from Easterton of Roseisle, Unstan and the Calf of Eday by Dr. Hans Helbaek and Professor Jessen of Denmark during the war (*Det kong. danske Videnskab. Selskab, Biol. Skrifter*, III, 2). The same grains have been identified on several Beakers, a couple of Food Vessels and many Cinerary Urns, and were therefore cultivated equally during stages III, IV, and V. Wheat-growing is not directly attested till the stage VI. Of course barley is better suited to northern climes than unselected wheats and makes excellent bread, as any one who has enjoyed bere scones in Orkney knows.

CHAPTER VI

THE CELTIC IRON AGE

THE introduction of iron into industry really did release new productive forces since for the first time it made efficient metal tools really cheap. The new material did not have to be imported from Ireland and Cornwall; it could be smelted almost anywhere from local ores, albeit of extremely poor quality. Save perhaps at Jarlshof no trace of prehistoric copper-smelting has been detected in Scotland; bloomeries for the production of iron have been found in Shetland, Aberdeenshire, the Hebrides, Skye, Fife, and the Lothians, while iron slag has been reported at other occupation sites.

All the bloomeries were no doubt exceedingly small so that each firing would yield only a tiny lump of iron. At Wiltrow, on a hill overlooking the shore settlement of Jarlshof, A. O. Curle[1] found a little furnace operated by a natural blast. Three narrow channels or flues, opening respectively to the north, east, and south, had been cleverly designed to catch the prevailing winds; the two on the leeward at any time could be closed by throttle slabs. But the best preserved channel, 4 ft. long, was only 5 or 6 inches wide and 4 to 5 inches high. Unfortunately the furnace proper was so dilapidated that neither its size nor structure could be determined. Bog ore was certainly smelted apparently with peat fuel.

In a cave near Rudh'an Dunain, Skye,[2] the blacksmith used a sort of Catalan forge, also apparently in pre-Roman times (Plate XV, 1). The hearth, an excavation in the peaty soil with slabs on edge to form sides and back, was $1\frac{1}{4}$ ft. deep and about 9 inches wide. It was found full of slag. Scott supposes that ore and charcoal were piled against the back and a blast directed on them from a bellows. A bloomery at Loanhead of Daviot,[3] dated early in stage VI by sherds of Old Keig ware, was marked only by well-baked soil and slag.

The remaining furnaces are probably no older than the Roman period. One in a beehive underground chamber in the fortified steading or manor at Castlelaw, Glencorse, was a mere pit in the rock floor about a foot across. In Constantine's Cave, Fife, on

[1] *Proc.*, lxx, 153.   [2] ibid., lxviii, 207.   [3] ibid., lxxi, 401.

80

the other hand, Jehu and Wace[1] found what sounds like a miniature blast furnace, but only the foundations survived. They were defined by two concentric rings of stones with clay between them surrounding a dished stone hearth with a cavity 15 inches across and three deep.

At each firing any of these furnaces should yield a small lump of spongy iron mixed with slag and charcoal. From this, by repeated hammering and heating, a little bloom of iron, perhaps 4 inches long and ½ inch thick, could be won eventually. Such formed the units from which iron implements could be built up and forged. Despite the long laborious process each community could now with luck obtain material for tools and weapons that would have been enormously cheaper, albeit often less efficient, than the bronze ones purveyed by travelling artificers or even cast by a resident bronze-smith.

Iron at last provided society with efficient axes for clearing the land that were more durable than stone ones and yet within the means of most farmers, and actually more efficient, too, than bronze celts. Even the early iron axe from Rahoy that still copies the socketed celt in form is heavier than any of these; it measures 7·12 inches long by 2·6 inches wide across the blade, while a bronze celt seldom exceeds 3·2 by 2·5 inches. From Dunagoil comes an axe of modern form with a transverse eyelet for the shaft and a blade 3 inches wide; similar but less reliably dated axes come from the Laws of Monifieth, Traprain Law,[2] and Buston crannog. The efficacy of these instruments for tree-felling is most directly indicated by the vast number of stout beams employed in a Gallic wall or a crannog. But their major significance was in opening up to tillage acres of woodland that stone axes were too fragile, and bronze ones too rare, to clear. Thanks to this agency sedentary communities of a quite unprecedented size were enabled to support themselves permanently in the great Gallic forts around the Tay estuary, in Strathmore, and between the Findhorn and the Beauly.

Iron tools probably contributed to the efficiency of tillage, too, but the proof is mainly inferential for pre-Roman Caledonia. The first iron ploughshare forms part of a hoard of largely Roman implements from Blackburn Mill, Berwickshire[3] (Plate XVI). Indeed, though the plough is far older than any iron ploughshare, there is no older positive evidence for plough cultivation in this country. I should like to claim the terraces below the broch of

---

[1] *Proc.*, xlix, 241.   [2] ibid., lv, 199.   [3] ibid., lxvi, 314–15.

6

Torwoodlee (Plate XV, 2 and Fig. 18)[1] as Celtic fields contemporary with the broch and so attributable to stage VIb, but Barger[2] thinks these terraces are of the strip type that may just as well be medieval. I do not believe that the corn undoubtedly consumed in Gallic forts and brochs could have been provided except from ploughed fields. In the Highlands, on the contrary, plough cultivation is not to be expected; the little plots actually associated with hut circles on our moors, whatever their date, are more appropriate to the hoe or at most the caschrom. For reaping the crop, iron sickles were freely used in England and on the Continent, but the Scottish specimens from Traprain Law and the crannogs are not demonstrably pre-Roman.

Indirectly intensified agriculture and an increased reliance on cereal foods are attested among all societies of stage VI, but their role in the rural economy was probably not the same everywhere. Among the broch-builders tillage was evidently a primary interest. The brochs are notoriously located on what is still regarded as the best arable land in Caithness and Orkney. Vast numbers of querns collected from their ruins graphically illustrate the heavy consumption of corn. But querns are everywhere conspicuous relics in stage VI. At the Gallic fort of Duntroon no less than 36 were found. All these belonged to the old saddle type in which the rubber is pushed to and fro. This type predominates in Gallic forts and occurs also in hill-top forts, brochs, and hut circles. But during stage VI the housewife's daily task was enormously lightened by the introduction of the rotary quern. This device, invented in the Mediterranean world somewhere before 400 B.C., gradually spread northward, reaching southern Britain perhaps by 100 B.C. A specimen from Lochlee crannog[3] approximates to the beehive type that is admittedly pre-Roman, but most are flatter and more like those used in the Highlands last century. Curwen[4] believes that in Britain such handmills were spread mainly by the Roman legionaries, but specimens have been found in the Gallic forts of Finavon and Dunagoil, and the type may have reached Scotland before Agricola's invasion, by Atlantic seaways ultimately from Spain, immediately in the wake of the broch-builders from south-western England.[5] Naturally it was only with the aid of iron tools and bolts that such mills could be carved and the two millstones pivoted together.

Judging by the very numerous bones from all domestic sites

[1] *Proc.*, lxvii, 75.　　[2] *English Historical Review*, 1938, 393.　　[3] Munro, p. 107.
[4] *Antiquity*, xi (1937), 148.　　　　　　　　　　　　　　[5] ibid., xvii (1945), 25.

including brochs, beef and mutton were as popular as ever. As before, the proportion of immature beasts is excessive among the cattle bones from Finavon, Dunagoil, and even Traprain. On the other hand, in the Gallic forts of Finavon, Abernethy, and Forgandenny, as in Shetland houses of stage VIa, numerous swine

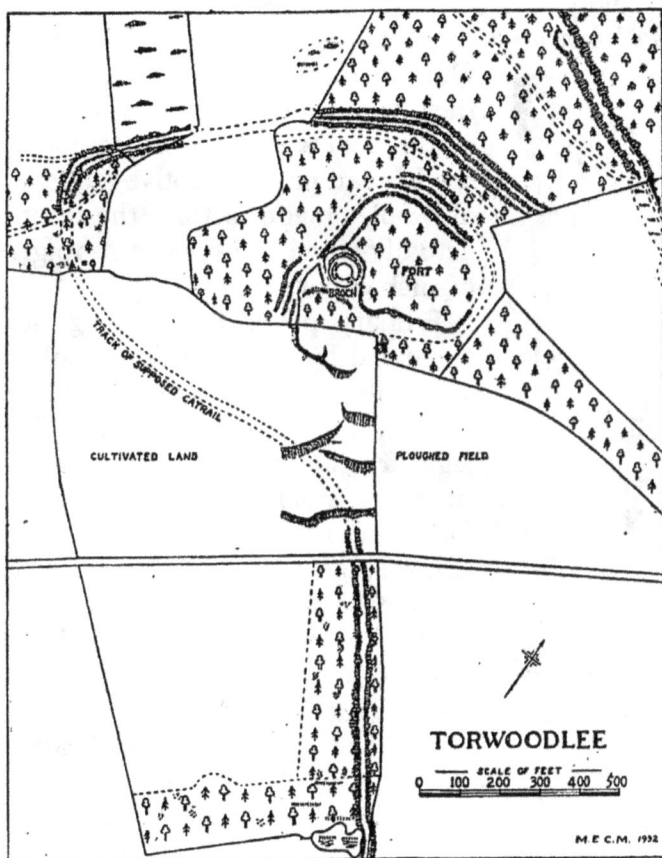

FIG. 18. PLAN OF ANCIENT FIELDS ROUND BROCH OF TORWOODLEE, AFTER MITCHELL AND JONES

bones indicate not only a taste for pork, but also a more sedentary life than prevailed in stages III to V. On the other hand, red and roe deer and wild fowl were still hunted and, of course, shell-fish and nuts were collected.

Iron shears from Traprain and the crannogs of Lochlee and Ashgrove Loch, though not certainly pre-Roman, imply that sheep were being bred for wool as well as meat and milk. In any case, stone spindle-whorls are among the commonest relics from all Iron Age sites; they indicate a flourishing textile industry. In the brochs immigrant women expanded this industry into a productive manufacture, using a specialized equipment of whorls made from femur-heads, long-handled combs of antler or whale-bone (Fig. 19), bobbins made from sheeps' metapodials, and other bone instruments that had been invented in south-western England before 100 B.C. Of course spinning and weaving were essentially household crafts plied primarily for domestic needs.

Only in the broch culture is it likely that they produced an exportable surplus and made wool a marketable commodity. By the Roman period a votive model of a bale of wool,[1] made within the Empire but actually found in Skye, seems to give proof of such exportation (Fig. 20).

Primary production having been thus expanded by the use of iron tools, Scottish soil could support a larger population than before. The domestic record of the Iron Age, fragmentary though it be, evidently denotes a much larger population than can be deduced from the funerary record of the Bronze Age. The individual dwellings are not indeed generally larger nor more commodious than some of stage II at Skara Brae or stage IV at Jarlshof. Apart from caves that offered refuges to some impoverished groups or outcasts, round houses or huts in the tradition already encountered in stage III near Muirkirk are the norm.

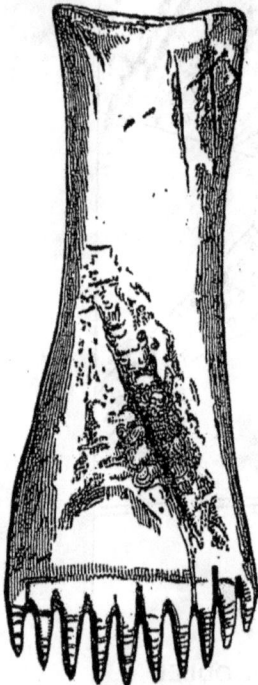

FIG. 19.   LONG-HANDLED WEAVING COMB, BROCH OF BURRIAN.   2/3

The best preserved buildings of this plan from pre-Roman times are the pre-broch hut-circles of Jarlshof and a wheel-house on the Calf of Eday (Fig. 11). Such measured 22 to 25 ft. in overall diameter. The living space seems to be obstructed by radial walls dividing the area into wedge-shaped compartments—nine in number and 4 to 5 ft. deep on Calf of Eday—round the central hearth. As only the bare foundations of the radial walls survive, it is impossible to say how completely they separated the compartments from one another. Their function may in any case have been primarily to take the place of the wooden posts that supported the radial rafters of the roof in wooded countries like

[1] *Proc.*, lxvi, 289, and xlix, 66; 20.

Wiltshire and Man. Better preserved dwellings of the same plan
survive from a later period at Jarlshof itself, on North Ronaldsay
and in the Outer Hebrides. But in no case is enough preserved
to decide whether the central space as well as the radial compartments was roofed while the exiguous furniture gives little clue
as to the functions of the compartments; but none were demonstrably cattle stalls. The wheel-house on the Calf of Eday seems
to have stood alone, but at Jarlshof at least two apparently
coexisted during stage VI and later examples form larger
groups.

Some of the innumerable
hut circles on the moors
of Sutherland, the central
Highlands, Aberdeenshire,
and even Galloway must
surely have been occupied
during stage VI. Excava-
tions in three or four examples have yielded querns,
potsherds, bits of iron or a
lignite bracelet that indicate
a vague Iron Age occupa-
tion, but have not fixed
their antiquity more pre-
cisely nor elucidated the

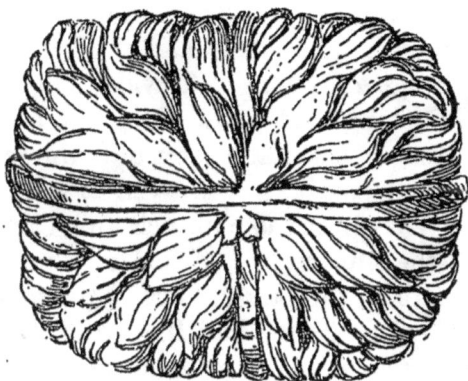

FIG. 20. ROMAN MERCHANT'S VOTIVE MODEL
OF A BALE OF WOOL, DUNANLARDHARD
BROCH, SKYE. ½

details of their structure or function. They occur in clusters,
comprising from two to twenty huts, with an average of six, nearly
always connected with small plots now defined by low turf banks.
There are eight such groups round the head-waters of the Ericht
and the Isla.[1] These cluster about the 1,000 ft. contour; but
farther north they are commoner at lower elevations; in Moray
and the Aird about 700, in Easter Sutherland round about 500 ft.
Obviously these exposed situations have been selected in order
to get above the denser forest, perhaps into the birchwood zones
—hardly above the prehistoric treeline altogether.

Finally, a crannog was probably essentially a round farm-house,
though on a more pretentious scale and built on an artificial
island. But none of the details of the actual dwelling have been
as yet laid bare in Scotland, and only one crannog has yet yielded
any plausibly pre-Roman relic—the handle of a typical Bronze
Age cauldron. Some were certainly post-Roman and without

[1] *Proc.*, lxvii, 189.

excavation such cannot be distinguished from those occupied in Roman times or earlier.

Attached even to the earliest wheel-house and to later dwellings of stage VIa at Jarlshof, as to those of the Hebrides, are curious subterranean chambers or galleries, technically termed 'earth-houses' or *souterrains*. Such are normally roofed with solid stone lintels supported by built walls. The earlier ones are absurdly low. The oldest, attached to dwelling IIIb at Jarlshof,[1] was a curved gallery, 13¾ ft. long, but at most 2½ ft. wide and about 2½ ft. high.[2] In the last reconstruction of this dwelling[3] the new earth-house boasted a chamber 11 ft. long and 4½ ft. wide, but still only 3 ft. high (Plate IX, 2). From dwelling VI[4] an underground passage 22 ft. long, 2 ft. wide, and only 2 ft. high led to a chamber 6 ft. long and 5 ft. wide, but apparently no higher than the passage. Even at a later date the maximum height of the souterrain at Foshigarry[5] is given as 3 ft.!

What were these tunnels for? Curle[6] suggests that the occupants of the hut-circles crawled up them to sleep in cold and stormy weather; the sandy floors of the galleries were found surprisingly clean, as if they had been protected by skins spread to serve as mattresses; in better weather the inhabitants would have slept under canopies in the supposedly unroofed circles in which comparable patches of clean sand were observed. I do not find this account convincing.

Now quite similar galleries of less restricted height are connected with extant hut circles in Easter Sutherland[7]—here the gallery was 5½ ft. high—and in the Dinnet group[8] in Aberdeenshire. Many more spacious souterrains have come to light without any vestige of the associated overground dwelling, that must be assumed in every case, in Orkney, Caithness, Sutherland, Aberdeenshire, Strathmore, Fife, and the Lothians. Some, south of the Forth, were admittedly not built till after A.D. 180, but one in Angus contained first-century Roman pottery and is therefore referrable to stage VI. Whatever their age all must be inspired by the same idea. They are just like air-raid shelters, and I believe fulfilled a similar purpose: they were funk-holes into which women and children could retreat and shelter in safety during a cattle-raid when the menfolk were away.

Lone steadings, hut-circle villages, and souterrains can give no adequate idea of the population of stage VI, since the numbers

[1] *Proc.*, lxviii, 238.   [2] ibid.   [3] ibid., 247.   [4] ibid., lxx, 241.
[5] ibid., lxv, 313.   [6] ibid., lxx, 247.   [7] ibid., xlv, 20.   [8] ibid., xxxviii, 112.

to be reckoned here cannot be estimated. Defensive constructions are better dated and give a more reliable impression. They fall into two contrasted groups. Wherever there are any extensive continuous tracts of cultivable plain, principally, therefore, in the east of Scotland, we find hill-tops occupied by forts large enough to accommodate a substantial force. Besides a few structures like Traprain Law, Burnswark, and Bonchester Hill, that can be dated independently, the most easily recognizable and best-dated group is constituted by the Gallic forts. On the other hand, in the West Highlands each isolated patch of arable in a glen or islet is dominated by a hill-top fort so small that it could only have held a single family. Among these, too, those constructed with Gallic walls are safely referrable to stage VI, but we have seen that the brochs farther north may be classed here too.

Now the mere construction of a large Gallic fort presupposes the employment of a substantial labour force. Finavon is a fairly typical specimen. The main citadel, perched on the summit of a steep conglomerate hill, was girt with a rampart that must have stood 12 to 16 ft. high, is still 25 ft. thick, and has a perimeter of some 333 yards. The faces of quarry-dressed sandstone blocks were tied together with timber lacings and the interspace filled with quarried stone and timber. Its construction involved the quarrying of more than 200,000 cubic feet of stone, while at least half as much timber must have been felled and cut up to provide the lacings. A terrace on the south side of the hill formed an outer bailey, 80 ft. wide, originally defended by a wall of comparable magnitude that no longer survives.[1] Moreover, two wells had been sunk through the solid rock, one to a depth of 20 ft.

The inner enclosure was about 100 ft. wide and some 500 ft. long, but, the ground being interrupted by two clefts, only 300 ft. of the length was fit for habitation. Excavation disclosed under the shelter of the north rampart, and so facing the sun, a row of dwellings the floors of which had been protected by debris from the rampart (Plate XIV, 2). The houses may have been rectangular; in any case, hearths occur at intervals of 25 ft. So there is room for a dozen in this row. The shady strip below the south rampart was devoted to industrial pursuits: potters' clay, spindle whorls, moulds, and crucibles were found there, but no domestic hearths. But there was room for at least one row of houses in the centre, where the soil is too thin for even foundations to survive.

[1] Jamieson in *Trans. R. Soc. Lit.* ii (1830), p. 242.

Cattle could, of course, be accommodated in the outer bailey. So there was room in the enceinte for 25 to 35 families—about as many as in a Neolithic village in Central Europe.

Finavon is representative of the group of larger Gallic forts— at least 24—of which two-thirds are situated on the eastern side of Scotland; but a few quite large forts—Dun Macuisneachan, Dunagoil, and Carradale—overlook some of the more extensive patches of fertile land in Lorne, Bute, and Kintyre. The contour forts of the Lowlands are of course larger. Traprain covers 32 acres, Burnswark 17, and Bonchester Hill 13. Not all the fortified spaces were built up, but trial excavations cannot reveal the density of habitation. At Traprain rectangular houses were inhabited in Roman times, but an early dwelling exposed under a secondary rampart in 1939 was just a hut-circle,[1] and circular huts were alone recognized on Bonchester Hill. All these monuments may then be called fortified villages or townlets; their scale alone would forbid the use of the term 'city'.

In the West Highlands the norm is quite different. At Rahoy the jagged summit of a crag overlooking Loch Teacuis was girt with a timber-laced stone rampart, nowhere less than 10 ft. thick, enclosing a roughly circular space 40 odd feet in diameter. To secure a level floor projecting bosses of rock had to be quarried away while hollows were filled loosely with lumps of rock and then covered over with timbers supporting a stamped earth floor. The central area was occupied by a pavement some 14 ft. across on the centre of which stood a rectangular hearth measuring 4½ ft. by 3½ ft. Beneath the floor some 10 ft. east of the hearth was an irregular chamber 5 ft. long and 3 to 5 ft. wide, roofed, a couple of feet above its rock bottom, by stout paving stones. Though a fierce conflagration had taken place within it distorting even its walls, it bears a suspicious resemblance to the souterrains of the north. The whole fortified area was, I believe, covered with a roof of turfs carried by rafters springing from the encircling rampart and supported at their inner ends by posts set round the hearth, the bases of two having been found.

The whole work perished in a terrific conflagration. The timber lacings of the rampart caught fire and burnt as in a kiln with such force that the rubble core filling the wall fused to a solid 'vitrified' mass, while the faces were burst apart by the expansion caused by the heat. Thereafter the floor timbers ignited, baking the earthen floor, while the blazing posts and

[1] *Proc.*, lxxiv, 54.

rafters fell, leaving the charred sods of the roof as a black layer above the debris of the rampart.

Enough remains to show that this grim structure on an isolated peak was no ordinary farm-house. No patriarchal family commanded the man-power to build such a fortress on such a spot. Rahoy was the castle of a chief. His retainers or clansmen who

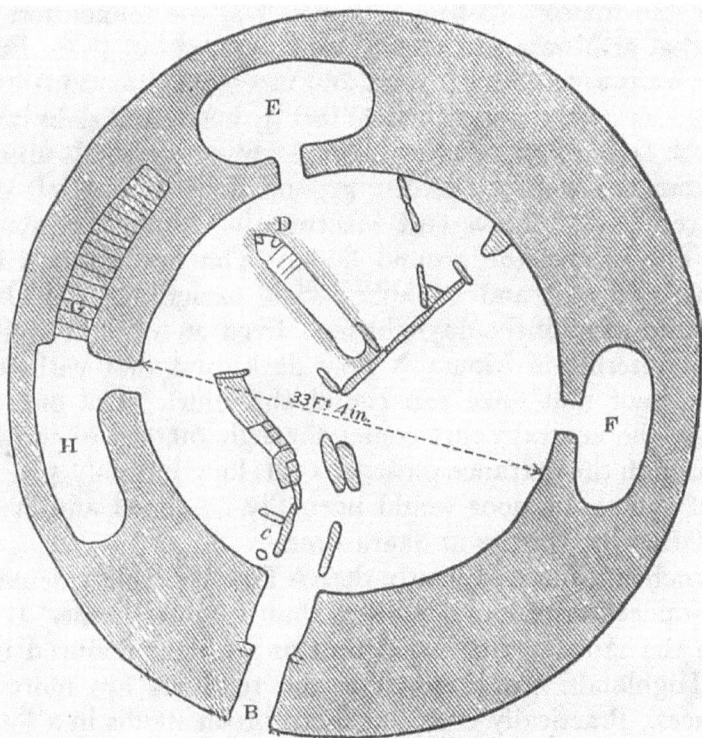

FIG. 21. BROCH OF THE MANSE OF HARRAY, ORKNEY:
GROUND FLOOR PLAN

did the building must in peacetime have lived outside the walls, presumably on holdings in the arable land beside the loch. About a dozen similar castles perched on isolated crags, on rocky promontories or tiny islands along the west coasts and Loch Fyne are likewise built with Gallic walls, now vitrified. Not all are round; some, e.g. at Onich, are rectilinear like Finavon. That at Onich must be a single rectangular house grown into a castle.

A like idea is expressed in a still more imposing form in the brochs, built rather later and perhaps to accommodate fresh invaders. The ground floor (Fig. 21) is just a big round house 30 to 40 ft. in diameter, save that its walls, 12 to 16 ft. in thickness, can accommodate three or four intramural chambers that are typically 8 to 12 ft. long, 4 or 5 ft. wide, and roofed with corbelled masonry 5 or more feet above the floor. Near the enclosure's centre is a large square hearth, and around it at Glenelg were seen the sockets for posts to support rafters springing from the wall. The court usually contains also a well or cistern cut in the living rock.

Now the massive six-foot wall was just the foundation for a tower that at Mousa was carried up to a height of 40 ft. But the tower's walls are no longer solid, but merely two concentric shells tied together every 4 or 5 vertical feet by horizontal slabs bonded into both faces. Between them a corkscrew stair winds up clockwise from the wall cell in the ground floor on the left of the entrance. (At Midhowe and Aikerness in Orkney[1] the staircase began only above the ground floor.) The result was a tower immensely strong and capable also of excluding even Orkney gales—and most of the daylight too. Even on a bright summer's day the interior of Mousa is very dark, and that without the veranda roof that once ran round the court. The only light reaching the central court comes through the top of the tower and through the entrance passage, 15 ft. long but only 4 ft. wide. And of course the door would normally be closed and fastened by a sliding bar, just as at Skara Brae.

A broch still more explicitly than a fort like Rahoy demanded the co-operation of more builders than it could house. It symbolizes the same sort of social unit as we have deduced in the West Highlands. And this time the retainers are more than inferences. Practically every northern broch stands in a fortified enclosure, and the space between the tower and the enceinte wall is crowded with small and rather flimsy hutments. The most conspicuous ones are often late additions, but the excavations at Aikerness (Gurness) proved that the oldest set, buried under subsequent reconstructions, was really contemporary with the tower.

Now a list just published by Graham[2] comprises over 500 probable or certain brochs. In Orkney alone 42 undoubted examples still stand, and there were probably 60 more; and on the Northern Mainland 172 or possibly 232. Such numbers must indicate a relatively dense population. And brochs are additional to, not substitutes for, other and presumably older types of settlement. Side by side with brochs, wheel-houses were inhabited in the Isles and hut-circles and souterrains in Easter Sutherland. In the same way hut-circle villages and the steadings to which

[1] *Proc.*, lxviii, 452.   [2] *Ant. J.*, xxiii, 19.

the extant earth-houses were attached must have co-existed with Gallic and contour forts in Aberdeenshire, Strathmore, and round the Tay.

The expanded population thus attested must have been supported almost entirely by farming and fishing. There had been little if any expansion of manufacture or commerce. The separation of handicraft from husbandry may indeed have been retarded or actually reversed. 'Superior tools have partially done away with the tyranny of the master craftsman,' writes Margaret Mead[1] of contemporary Samoa. With iron knives and axes farmers could make at home household appliances that would demand an expert's skill to fashion with stone tools. All pottery was still built up by hand without the use of the wheel, as in previous stages. Old Keig ware and cognate fabrics from Jarlshof and Traprain are indeed better fired than Cinerary Urns. But the domestic pottery from Bonchester Hill and the Gallic forts of Abernethy, Dunagoil, and Finavon is inferior even to Late Bronze Age urns and owes nothing to the Bronze Age tradition; it gives the impression of having been made by inexpert foreign women who did not know where to find the best clay. There is no more evidence for the industrialization of the ceramic industry than in stage II. The conversion of a wheel-house on the Calf of Eday to serve in its last days as a 'potter's workshop' implies no more than the kilns of Eilean an Tighe.

Probably wooden and steatite vessels that could be easily carved with iron knives took the place of earthenware for many purposes. Remains of wooden bowls and ladles were found in the Gallic fort at Abernethy, as well as in many crannogs; steatite ladles occur not only in brochs, but at Dunagoil and the Hyndford crannog. No pottery at all was used at Rahoy.

Metal-working was presumably still a specialist's job, but perhaps not so exclusively as in the Bronze Age. Indications of iron-working have been recorded from crannogs, brochs, and lone steadings, as well as from large hill-top forts. Bronze, too, was still worked. Crucibles for melting it, stone moulds for bars, and clay moulds for pins or spear-butts are found in most types of settlement. Moreover, the bronze-smith continued casting swords and axes after iron-smelting had started at Jarlshof, while moulds for swords and actual axes of bronze were found on Traprain. The iron axes forged in imitation of cast bronze celts from Traprain, Rahoy, and Bishops Loch must mean that bronze and iron

[1] *Coming of Age in Samoa.*

were in competition during much of stage VI. Indeed, Anderson inferred from a bronze celt found in the Roman camp at Ardoch that such implements were still in use after the end of stage VI.

Presumably all these smiths were residents. Evidently they were largely recruited from the Bronze Age artisans who had begun to settle down towards the end of stage V. But one wonders whether a broch community, for example, could afford to support a resident smith. The highly skilled artist craftsmen who fashioned superb objects of parade like the Torrs chamfrein, if they visited Caledonia at all in stage VI, would of course have come as the guests of prosperous local chieftains and landlords. Incidentally, it should be remarked that iron provided the smiths of Traprain and the crannogs with proper hinged tongs for the first time.

There must have been some other crafts; rotary querns, for instance, must have been made by specialists, and expert wheelwrights would be needed to fashion war chariots. But of these the archaeological record says nothing.

The possibility of obtaining almost anywhere, albeit from miserably poor ores, enough iron for the essential weapons and indispensable tools allowed to each local group a degree of self-sufficiency impossible in the Bronze Age. Indeed, the extreme difficulty of dating the hut-circles on our moors may be due to their inhabitants' acquiescence in a Neolithic isolation. The only trade explicitly attested in stage VI was directed to satisfaction of demands for ornaments and objects of parade—lignite armlets, and brooches, pins, bracelets, and spear-butts of bronze. This was accordingly a luxury trade to meet the desires of those who commanded the social surplus. They could be satisfied by the distributive mechanism elaborated in the Bronze Age and by the same personnel. First in the Roman period—and even then only in the partially subjugated Lowlands—do hoards like that from Blackburn Mill illustrate trade in productive tools, apparently manufactured in larger workshops within the civilized Province.

It would accordingly be quite wrong to regard a Gallic or contour fort as anything remotely approaching an Oriental city of the Bronze Age, a Greek *polis*, or a Roman municipality. It housed no bourgeoisie of artisans and merchants, still less of clerks or civil servants. The residents within its walls presumably tilled plots within walking distance of the hill-top, and grazed their livestock on adjacent uplands. If farmers from a wider area took refuge within the enceinte in time of war, they need not repair thither in peacetime to replenish their stocks; even iron seems to have been produced in hamlets and lone steadings, as already pointed out. In the West Highlands and the Northern Isles, of course, society had not progressed even this far.

Indeed, the best attested industry in stage VI, apart from farming, is war, the production of illth. It is true that weapons figure less prominently among the relics of the Iron Age than in earlier stages; only a few spear-heads and sword blades have survived corrosion. Tacitus reports that the Britons under Galgacus employed war-chariots in A.D. 84, and from the first and succeeding centuries plenty of paired bits and harness mountings confirm his statement archaeologically. But the best archaeo-logical evidence for chariots in stage VI is a terret from the broch of Tor-woodlee (Fig. 22). Some transversely pierced tines from Dunagoil may be cheekpieces from bits of the old Bronze Age-Hallstatt pattern that had been superseded on the Continent and in Yorkshire by bits with terminal rings by 200 B.C., but may equally well be knife-handles.

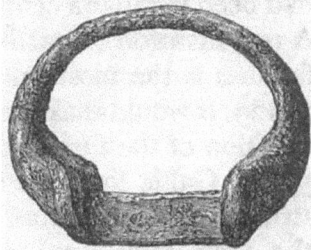

FIG. 22. BRONZE TERRET BROCH OF TORWOODLEE. $\frac{2}{3}$

The horse is conspicuously absent from the lists of fauna—mostly food-refuse—collected at the early sites of Abernethy, Dunagoil, Finavon, and Forgandenny. But of course people don't eat their war-horses. Despite the absence of positive evidence chariotry in Scotland should be as old as the Gallic wall and the safety-pin. Now even with iron tools a chariot would have been a relatively costly engine in a poor society. The horses specially trained to draw it, must have cost still more. Not so the remaining weapons. Every farmer could afford an iron spear as much as an iron axe.

Cheap iron had, in fact, released new forces of destruction as well as of production and made formidable weapons as generally available as efficient tools. If most of these have rusted away, the subterranean refuges attached to farms and still more the tremendous defences of forts and castles are eloquent testimony to a state of perpetual war. It was the need for protection that rove men to settle on exposed hill-tops and produced whateverd social consolidation was achieved. As in stage V, the favourite way of acquiring wealth was to seize what others had made, bred, or grown. And by the same token farmers' younger sons, for whom there was no room at home, could acquire land that other hands had cleared.

In the Lowlands, round Stirling, on the Gala Water, and on the Lammermuirs there are half a dozen isolated brochs reproducing all the distinctive features of the northern towers. They must represent colonies planted by the prolific populations of the North that may well have been becoming congested judging from the figures cited above.

Most probably the brochs and even the Gallic forts are memorials of a similar acquisition of Scottish soil by invaders impelled by comparable aims. In the brochs men and women used for the first time in Scotland a whole series of devices— textile appliances, triangular crucibles, dice, ornaments—that had been familiar a century or so earlier in south-western England. A real invasion of warlike chieftains with their retainers and their families is the most reasonable deduction. And as explained on p. 129, it would make intelligible Orosius' curious reference to the addition of the Orkneys to the Roman Empire in A.D. 43.

The Gallic forts are defended by walls of a pattern and constructed by techniques developed and perfected earlier, during the First Iron Age, in Gaul. Their occupants favoured new fashions of dress, strange to the Bronze Age, requiring brooches. The brooches themselves represent the culmination of a long evolutionary process, all the earlier stages of which can be traced over a thousand years on the Continent. The pottery from these forts owes nothing to Bronze Age traditions. The locations of many, overlooking the Tay estuary, Montrose harbour, and the Moray Firth, would be convenient for invaders who had arrived from beyond the North Sea. (Nevertheless ring-head pins are distinctively British, the iron axe from Rahoy copies the local Bronze Age form, and this castle itself preserves the plan of the native round house.)

If, then, these monuments be indeed the work of invaders, these would have come to appropriate Scottish soil from overseas, as in stage V Urn-folk may have set out from Galloway to seize land in Ireland and as some broch-folk later did occupy territory in the Lowlands. Now if you can thus acquire land by the same respectable methods of collective robbery as acquired cattle and commodity wealth, land itself may come to be regarded as a commodity, a possession. It can then be owned—even privately owned—and the last vestige of primitive communism will have vanished.

Now, as explained, the little Gallic forts of the West Highlands were the castles of chiefs—successors to the sacred chiefs who had led the clans in stage IV and there may not have disappeared in stage V. But the new Iron Age chief who has acquired his rank by force of arms may be regarded as owner of the land dominated and protected by his castle. Its cultivators would by the same token be tenants; their traditional dues and services may become rents. Still more patently is the broch the castle of a chief who from his tower, like a Norman baron from his keep, dominates the old native population, who live on in their wheel-houses and hut-circles. In so far as the broch-lord be also a landlord, the natives will be his serfs.

There is no evidence that the larger Gallic forts were chieftains' residences; neither princely gear nor palace foundations have been found therein, but without total excavation of a typical site no final inference can be drawn. The literary references to Celtic society would be compatible with the view that such forts were miniature republics. Even so, their occupants would, as conquerors, constitute an aristocracy claiming ownership over the land they had won and rent and services from such of the earlier population as they had not massacred or enslaved, but left to till the ground from their hut-villages and souterrains. They would thus be able to annex a surplus for the upkeep of their chariots and the payment of the craftsmen who fashioned their brooches and horse-trappings.

So by stage VI we have passed from the primitive communism of stage II to a society divided into classes—but still an illiterate and barbarian society. A small class of war-chiefs and charioteers does now concentrate a social surplus. There are too many of them to collect much in so poor a land. And, having acquired it by force, they expend it on armaments and objects of parade and not on reproductive works. Such relations of production are merely fetters to the development of productive forces.

Still such an economic system may persist indefinitely. Loot may cover up the deficiencies of the productive mechanism and heroic deaths in battle may relieve the pressure on the land. But its principal beneficiaries are liable to be its most hapless victims. In Scotland the vitrified ruins of the Gallic forts tell of the overthrow of their builders by the Romans, or perhaps by the same invaders who built the brochs. The Brythonic aristocracy that built the forts and castles and left the place-names recorded by

Ptolemy, in so far as they survived the Roman onslaught, succumbed to Goidel, Norseman, Saxon, and Norman. Under the aegis of the latter a progressive class for which the hill fort had no room found somewhat grudging shelter till in the end it bought out the landed aristocracies.

APPENDICES

I. THE TYPOLOGY OF CHAMBERED CAIRNS AND THEIR CONTENTS

THE distinctive features of the several groups are as follows:

(*A*) All the 24 cairns from Shetland seem to be round cairns standing on a heel-shaped platform.[1] Fifteen covered a cruciform chamber entered by a passage from the concave base of the 'heel'.

(*B*) In the Old Red Sandstone region of Orkney and Caithness the cairns cover chambers built of the flat slabs into which the local rock breaks so easily, and roofed by corbelling. Most are subdivided by pairs of upright slabs and all are entered by a passage lower and narrower than the chamber. B1.—In Caithness and in five or six Orkney tombs two pairs of uprights projecting from the side walls divide the chamber into three compartments. Eleven of the cairns in Caithness and two in Orkney are long and horned, while four are short horned. B2.—The stalled cairns (Plate IV, 1) resemble the foregoing save that the chamber comprises more than three compartments, the maximum number being twelve (No. 33), while in one instance (38) the passage is at right angles to the major axis of the chamber. B3.—The passage is again at right angles to the chamber and the divisional slabs project from the back wall only. B4.—Instead of the chamber being divided into compartments, small lateral cells three to thirteen in number open off it. Six chambers of types B3 and B4 (39, 49, 57, 58, 66, 67) have been built partly in an excavation quarried on a hill-side. In two such (39, 49) a second chamber entered by a distinct passage has been built upon the roof of the first.

(*C*) In Sutherland and Ross and in the Western Isles the rock is less suitable for dry stone building, so that the chamber walls have to be formed mainly of upright slabs.

(*D*) The distinctive features of all Clava tombs are a roughly circular chamber defined by rounded boulders on edge which once supported corbelled masonry, covered by a round cairn defined by a peristalith of similar boulders surrounded by a ring of free-standing uprights. In at least eight cases in Black Isle, Glen Urquhart, the Nairn Valley, and Strathspey the chamber was entered by a narrow passage, but in others, equally widely distributed, it was completely closed. The uprights are often adorned with cup-marks.

(*E*) The chamber consists of a long cist framed by two parallel rows of slabs on edge supporting corbelled masonry. It is normally divided into segments by low transverse slabs, termed septal stones, and opens

[1] Bryce, *Proc.*, lxxiv, 23-36.

without any preceding passage through a pair of portal stones on to the exterior of the cairn. This is normally wedge-shaped and up to 120 feet long. In eight cases termed *horned cairns*, the portal stones are the tallest members of a semicircle of uprights forming a concave façade at the wide end. But sometimes more than one cist is covered by the same cairn.

(F) The chambers are cists, but consist of one segment only, and are entered generally across a threshold stone through a distinct built passage. The cairns may be long and in three cases are horned, the axial chamber opening on to a semicircular forecourt. But cairns in the Solway group normally cover more than one chamber, there being five in some instances.

In 1934 I proposed to divide Scottish megalithic tombs into passage graves in the north and long cists in the south-west, and so to construct two contrasted cultures. The two types would have divergent relations in Eire and on the Continent, and were further distinguished by their ceramic content—Unstan and Beacharra ware (Plate I) respectively. But the supposed duality of the megalithic tradition must be taken with reserve. Most 'cists' of the Solway group in Galloway and Ayrshire were actually entered through passages that might attain a length of 22 feet (342). The chamber at Achnacree (281), though entered by a long passage, roofed by corbelling and covered by a round cairn, is cist-like in plan. At Clettraval (253) the chamber is a quadrangular termination to a passage that grows wider and higher from its mouth and is subdivided by threshold slabs very much like the septal stones of a Clyde segmented cist. So in Ross some chambers are formed of parallel lateral slabs and are distinguished from the passages more by height than anything else. Finally, an Orcadian stalled cairn is in plan just a cist in which the segmentation is effected by paired uprights instead of transverse septal stones. Nor can the alleged contrast in ceramic furniture be rigidly upheld. The largest collections of Beacharra vases actually come not from Clyde cists, but from the passage graves of Unival and Clettraval (Plate I, 2) in North Uist, while a sherd from a stalled cairn on Eday (53) is decorated in channelled technique proper to Beacharra, though it is too small for the pattern or composition to be determined. And hence, for our purposes the megalithic complex can be treated as a unit and the sub-groups previously indicated may be taken as the results of divergent development of a common tradition, stimulated, perhaps, by different external 'influences' and differences in the mesolithic background.

Only sixty-six of these cairns have been excavated at all systematically and only thirty-five have yielded any significant relics whatsoever. No tomb of the Clava or Solway type, nor any of the Quoyness variety, has yielded any relics, so that the status of these groups is dubious. But in representative tombs of all the remaining groups excavation has disclosed furniture including typical 'neolithic pottery' (twenty-four tombs) and stone axes (six tombs) and leaf-shaped arrowheads. On the other hand, no less than ten tombs (37, 87, 106, 111, 253, 254, 275, 285, 286, 304), equally widely distributed, contained also sherds of the Beaker pottery that defines stage III for us. Nevertheless, the conditions of the finds at least in Nos. 106, 253, 254, and 285, leave no possibility of doubt that the Beakers were associated only with the latest interments in the vaults.

Everywhere we find the same leathery Atlantic or Western pottery allied to the Windmill Hill ware of southern England, and often the same specialized variants on it. So rolled-over and squashed-down rims can be cited from Orkney to Arran (56, 63, 111, 281, 297, 304). Keeled vessels with everted rim seem indeed to be confined to the northern groups, but the 'baggy pot with lugs', though commonest in the west (300, 301, 302, 314, 253), has now turned up in Orkney too (41). And finger-tip fluting is represented round L. Fyne and L. Etive, as well as in Strathspey and Moray.

LIST OF CHAMBERED CAIRNS

From my complete list of 357 examples the most important only will be recorded here with their original numbers and references to the rest merely indicated.

B, or B ware, Beacharra ware; Bkr., Beaker; U. Unstan ware; W. plain Western pottery.

1-24	SHETLAND, A., R.C. *Shetland.*
25-7	Westray, R.C. *Orkney,* and so for other numbers to 72 save.
28	Holm of Papa Westray, B4, 14 cells, *Arch.,* xxxiv, 123.
30	Quoyness, Sanday, B4, 6 cells, 15 skels., *Proc.,* vii, 398.
33	Midhowe, Rousay, B2, 12 comps., 25 skels., U., *Proc.,* lxviii, 320.
35	Lairo, B1, long horned, stone axe, *Proc.,* lxxvii, 155.
37	Yarso, B2, 4 comps., 29 skels., ? Bkr., *Proc.,* lxix, 325.
38	Blackhammer, B2, 7 comps., 2 skels., U., axe, *Proc.,* lxxi, 297.
39	Taiverso Tuack, two-storied chamber, upper B3, *Proc.,* lxxiii, 155; lower B3, 3 comps., U., *Proc.,* xxxvii, 77.
41	Craie, B1, W. pottery, unpublished.
49	Huntersquoy, Eday, two-storied chamber, upper B3, axe; lower B3, *Proc.,* lxxii, 193.
53	Sandyhill Smithy, lower B1, ? B. ware, *Proc.,* lxxii, 204.
56	Calf of Eday, B2, U., *Proc.,* lxxi, 134.
63	Unstan, Stromness, B3, U., a. hs., flint knife polished, *Proc.,* xix, 349.
73-86	CAITHNESS, R.C. *Caithness,* and so for other numbers to 135, except
87	Lower Dounreay, B1, horned, 5 skels., axe, Bkr. secondary, *Proc.,* lxiii, 138.

105   Yarrows, B1, long horned, *Mem. Anthr. Soc.*, ii, 237.
106   Yarrows, B1, long horned, secondary Bkr. in cist.
111   Kenny's Cairn, round, bipartite with lateral cell, U., rusticated and corded wares, *Mem. Anthr. Soc.*, iii, 227.
112   Ormiegill, short horned, tripartite, 30 skels., mace, *Mem. Anthr. Soc.*, iii, 243.
113   Cairn of Get, short horned, tripartite, 8 skels., *Mem. Anthr. Soc.*, iii, 218.
116   Camster, round, B1, rusticated ware, iron knife, *Mem. Anthr. Soc.*, ii, 248.
149–77 SUTHERLAND, C1, R.C. *Sutherland*.
178–202 ROSS and northern Inverness, C1, *Proc.*, lxxviii, 26–37.
203–4   BANFFS AND ABERDEENSHIRE, C1 ?, *Proc.*, lix, 26.
205–10 BLACK ISLE, Beauly valley, Glen Urquhart, D., *Proc.*, xvi, 312, 478; lxxviii, 37–9.
212–31 Ness and Nairn valleys, D., *Proc.*, xviii, 330–56.
232–7   Speyside, D., *Proc.*, xl, 245; xliv, 200.
239–78 WESTERN ISLES AND SKYE, C2, R.C. *Skye and the Hebrides*, except
253   Clettraval, N. Uist, long, 'segmented passage-grave', B. ware, secondary Bkr., *Proc.*, lxix, 482.
254   Unival, N. Uist, B. ware, Skara Brae and Bkr. secondary, unpublished.
275   Rudh'an Dunain, Skye, horned, C2, W. pottery, *Proc.*, lxvi, 188.
281   Achnacree, L. Etive, Lorne, round, segmented chamber, W., *Proc.*, ix, 411.
285   Nether Largie, Kilmartin, round, E., 4 segs., W., secondary Bkr., *Proc.*, vi, 340.
286   Kilchoan, Poltalloch, E., W., secondary Bkr., *Proc.*, vi, 351.
287–91 Loch Fyne, E., *Proc.*, lxvi, 455 and 205; lxxvii, 32.
292   Holy Loch, E., *Proc.*, xliii, 365.
294   Blochcairn, Baldernoch, STIR., Ure, *Rutherglen and Kilbride*, 87.
295–6   BUTE, E., *Proc.*, xxxviii, 27–37.
297   Glecknabae, Bute, 2 cists, E., 1 seg., B. ware, *Proc.*, xxxviii, 3.
298   Bickers Houses, Bute, E., 3 segs., B. ware, *Proc.*, xxxviii, 18.
299   Carn Ban, Arran, horned, E., 4 segs., *Proc.*, xxxvii, 40.
300   Torlin, Arran, E., 4 segs., 8 skels., *Proc.*, xxxvi, 79.
301   Clachaig, Arran (2 cists), E., 2 segs., 14 skels., B. ware, axe, *Proc.*, xxxvi, 90.
302   Sliddery Water (2 cists), E., 3 segs., W. ware, *Proc.*, xxxvi, 92.
303   Tormore, Arran, E., 3 segs., mace, *Proc.*, xxxvi, 98.
304   Giants' Graves, Arran, horned, E., 4 segs., ? Bkr., *Proc.*, xxxvii, 45.
305–13 ARRAN, E., Bryce, *The Book of Arran*, except
311   Dunan Beag, Blairmore, 2 cists, E., 2 segs., 3 skels., B. and ? FV. wares, *Proc.*, xliii, 348.

312   Dunan Mor, Blairmore, 2 cists, 2 and 3 segs. resp., *Proc.*, xliii, 351.

314   Beacharra, Kintyre, E., 3 segs., B. ware, *Proc.*, xxxvi, 103.

315–19 KINTYRE AND GIGHA.

320–1   ISLAY, *Proc.*, xxxvi, 110.

322–7   AYRSHIRE, F., *Proc.*, xi, 278; lxxvii, 33; Smith, *Prehistoric Man in Ayrshire.*

328–33 WIGTONSHIRE, F., R.C. *Wigtons.*

334–41 KIRKCUDBRIGHTSHIRE, F., R.C. *Kirkcudbrights.*

342   Kings Cairn, Water of Deugh, round, F. 2 cists with pass., *Proc.*, lxiv, 273.

343–9   DUMFRIESSHIRE, uncertain types, R.C. *Dumf.*

350   Mutiny Stones, Berwicks.

351   Kindrochat, Comrie, on Earn, ? 3 cists, a.h., *Proc.*, lxv, 281.

352–5   TAY BASIN, unclassifiable, *Proc.*, lxxvii, 31; xlv, 98.

355–7   KINCARDINE AND ABERDEENSHIRES, *Proc.*, lviii, 23; lix, 21.

II. THE TYPOLOGY OF BEAKERS

Dr. Crichton-Mitchell published a list of Beakers in *Proceedings*, lxviii, 1934, and her numbering is used in the sequel. In calculating the number of Beaker-burials her Nos. 93–7, 100–8, 156–87, 192, 196–8, 277–90, have been omitted, being derived from domestic sites. The following new Beaker-burials have come to light since 1934:

ci., cist; sk., skeleton; M., male; F., female.

ABERDEENSHIRE

15a   CA, Newlands, Oyne, ci., sk., 2 wrist-guards and a. hs., *Proc.*, lxx, 331.

12a   CB, Blackhills, Skene, ci., sk., *Proc.*, lxviii, 415.

10a   CB, Rathen, Fraserburgh, ci., in 'mound', *Proc.*, lxix, 382.

42a   CA, Upper Boyndlie, Tyrie, ci., ? sk., *Proc.*, lxvii, 185.

36a   C, Kemnay, Donside, sk., F., *Proc.*, lxxi, 367.

37a   CA, Boghead, Pitsligo, ci., *Proc.*, lxxvii, 187.

67a   Frag. Loanhead, Daviot, from Stone Circle, *Proc.*, lxix, 173.

68b   B (ornamented w. continuous cord), Kintore, at Halliburton House.

ANGUS

71a   CB, Lunanhead, Forfar, in paved cist, sk., M., *Proc.*, lxxvi, 129.

72a   Burnside, Kirkbuddo, ci., acquired N.M.A., October 1944.

72b   Kirkbuddo.

AYRSHIRE

101a   Frag., Beoch, Dalmellington, on edge of cairn, *Proc.*, lxxii, 241.

102a   B (corded), Boreland, Old Cumnock, *Proc.*, lxxiv, 136.

CAITHNESS
148a   CB, Glengolly, Thurso, *Proc.*, lxix, 116.
EAST LOTHIAN
154a   CA, Nunraw, Garwald, ci., sk. (child), *Proc.*, lxxviii, 116.
156a   CA, West Fenton, Dirleton, ci., *ibid.*
189a   CA, Thurston Mains, Innerwick, ci., 2 skels., F., *Proc.*, lxxiv, 140
190a   CA, Thornton, Innerwick, ci., sk. (child), *Proc.*, lxxiii, 319.
191a   CA, W. Pinkerton, Dunbar, ci., 2 skels., M., *Proc.*, lxxiii, 232.
FIFE
195a   B corded, Brackmont Mill, Leuchars, in sandpit, *Proc.*, lxxvi, 86.
202a   C, Kirkcaldy, ci., sk., *Proc.*, lxxviii, 109.
INVERNESS
203a   CA, Lochend, Inverness, ci., sk., M., *Proc.*, lxxviii, 106.
206a   Clettraval, North Uist, with secondaries in chambered cairn, *Proc.*, lxix, 519.
207a   Unival, North Uist, with secondaries in chambered cairn, unpublished.
ROSS
256a   CB, Findon, Black Isle, ci., *Proc.*, lxxi, 248.
SUTHERLAND
273a   CA, Strathnaver, *Proc.*, lxviii, 473.

In England at least three groups of invaders can now be distinguished by varieties of Beakers—types A, B1, and B2 respectively—by the relics associated with them, and by their divergent distributions. In Scotland these distinctions are hardly relevant. The vast majority of Scottish Beakers belong to the degeneration of the A group, traditionally termed type C. It is true that by a minute analysis of forms and ornaments Dr. Crichton-Mitchell distinguished degenerations of B beakers (Cb) from degenerations of As (Ca). But they do not define distinct cultures in Scotland. In four instances (her nos. 3, 5, 14, 130) Ca and Cb beakers were found together in the same cist grave. Wrist-guards, in England distinctive of group B1, have been found in Scotland associated equally with Cb (8, 15a) and Ca (56, 89) beakers (Plate V, 2). True B beakers, generally ornamented with continuous cord impressions, certainly stand out from the general run of Cs. They are widely scattered from John o' Groats to Dunbar and from Mull to Glenluce. From their occurrence in collective tombs in Caithness (87, 106) and (probably) Arran (304 and 311) and in association with 'overlap pottery' at Drumelzier (246) and in the Muirkirk hut-circles, it might seem that such are early in Scotland as in England. On the other hand, in at least two graves B beakers were associated with 'jet' necklaces, and that not only of the disc (149a), but also of the crescentic, type (194), which are more often associated with Food Vessels in stage IV, and in any case accompany normal C beakers too. Moreover, some have a collar below the rim (Plate V, 3)

(68, 99, 117, 202a), a feature which, although paralleled in Holland, seems in Scotland generally late, perhaps a prelude to the Cinerary Urn. For our purposes Beakers denote a single society that ultimately occupied the whole of Scotland.

But they need not represent a single period of time, nor perhaps even a single stage in social evolution. While a chronological overlap with stage II may be deduced from the discovery of Beakers in chambered cairns, there are no less clear indications that some Beakers were contemporary with Food Vessels of stage IV. Beakers Nos. 8, 194, were, as remarked, associated with jet necklaces more commonly accompanying Food Vessels. The bronze armlets found with Beaker 228 in Lanarkshire are identical with those buried with Food Vessel 53 in Kincardineshire. Five Beakers from North-east Scotland (3, 4, 10, 11, 112) and one from Mull (89) have internally bevelled rims clearly copied from Food Vessels (Plate V, 4) (*Proc.*, xliii, 91). Others (e.g. 77, 78) can only be described as Beaker Food-Vessel hybrids. Incidentally No. 78, like No. 209, accompanied cremated bones, but cremation is more appropriate to the Food Vessel complex.

III. RECUMBENT STONE CIRCLES

Such are confined to North-east Scotland where over seventy are known (Fig. 23). Most have been violated, some even in prehistoric times. Cremated remains were found within the circles of Hatton of Ardoyne (*Proc.*, xxxv, 241), Castle Fraser (xxxv, 198), Esslie (xxxiv, 162), Seanhinney (xxxiv, 181), Strone (xxxvi, 493), Candle Hill (xxxvi, 529), and Ardlair (xxxvi, 557) by amateur diggings and by more scientific excavation in Garrol Wood, Old Keig (lxviii, 372), and Loanhead of Daviot (lxix, 168), in the last two with traces of the pyre. Beaker sherds were obtained from Old Keig and Loanhead and a wrist-guard from Old Rayne (xxxvi, 530), but not demonstrably in association with any interment. Flat-rimmed urns, here assigned to stage VI, were common both at Old Keig and Loanhead.

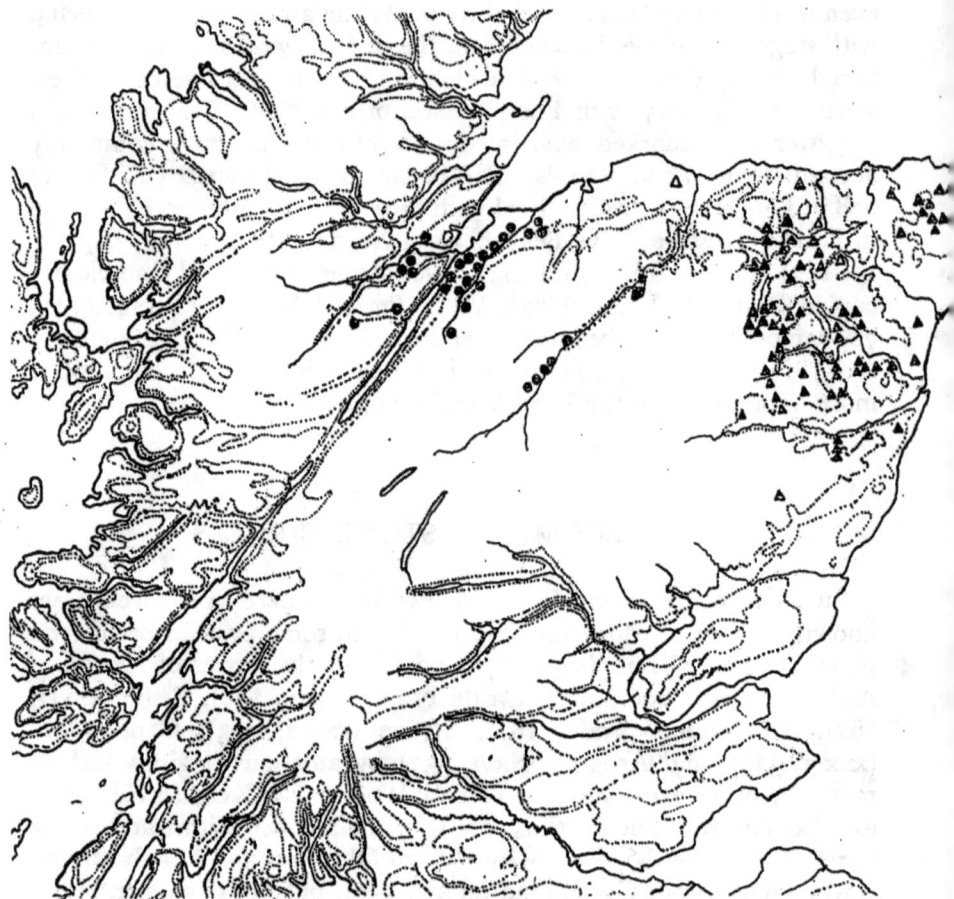

FIG. 23. DISTRIBUTION OF CHAMBERED CAIRNS OF CLAVA TYPE (DOTS) AND A RECUMBENT STONE CIRCLES (TRIANGLES).

IV. CLASSIFICATION OF FOOD VESSELS

In type B the body is an inverted truncated cone separated by a sharp shoulder from a concave neck surmounted by an everted rim. The shoulder is often grooved (B1), sometimes doubly grooved (B2), and the grooves may be spanned by stop-ridges, pierced (B1a, B2a), or unpierced (B1b, B2b). The commonest decoration is composed of horizontal zones of herring-bone motives executed with a comb-like stamp (hr). Type A (Plate VII, 1) is a bowl-shaped vessel with no distinct neck nor shoulder and no eversion, but rather inversion of the rim. The ornamentation is often arranged vertically, sometimes in panels; false relief (FR) is used on nine (45 per cent) as against only some ten Bs (10 per cent). In type C (Plate VII, 2) the body is inverted conical, as in B, but the neck is not concave nor is the rim everted. The shoulder is emphasized by from one (C1) to six (C6) ribs. Plainly, the distinctions between C1 and simple B, C2, and B1, and C3 and B2 are very fine and often doubtful. False relief is used in some ten instances.

Seven As, one-third of the total, come from the Clyde Firth province and the west coast of Argyll, where they account for 17·6 per cent of recorded Food Vessels. But three out of fourteen Food Vessels from North-east Scotland are As. Twelve Cs come from the Clyde Firth and Argyll, seven from the Clyde Valley, and three from Galloway, accounting respectively for 31·6, 30, and 21·3 per cent of the classifiable Food Vessels, but there are five between Dee and Tay and four from the Lothians. Nine As, no less than 47·6 per cent of the total, accompanied cremated remains, whereas of all ascertainable Food Vessel burials only 21 per cent were after cremation. The proportion of Cs with cremations does not exceed the average. No distinctive relics have been found with A bowls. Vases of type C may be accompanied by crescentic jet necklaces, etc., as much as other Food Vessels.

It follows that there is no excuse for creating distinct cultures to be defined by types A, B, and C, still less for postulating an invasion from Ireland to explain A. It will appear in the sequel that type A is in general later than B, rather than earlier, as Abercromby and his successors, including the author, thought.

LIST OF FOOD VESSELS

	Type	Ornament	Burial Rite	Associations	
NORTH OF BEAULY FIRTH					
2 Apigill Junc., Strathnaver	—	—	ci.	jet cresc.	Proc., 73, 326
3 Sordale Hill, Thurso	B1	co.	?	niche in wall of megalithic chamber	,, 43, 19
4 Acoilemore, Brora	?	c	—	ci.	,, 74, 22
5 Torrish, Kildonan	B	—		in ca. a.h.	,, 8, 408
6 Strathfleet	?	mg.	sk.	a.h.	,, 8, 50
7–8 Brora	B1	—	—	ci.	,, 45, 317
9 Achinchanter, Dornoch	B1a	hr.	—	ci. a.h.	,, 74, 14
10 ,, ,,	—	—	—	ci.	
11 Balblair, Edderton	0	0	—	ci. cres. fl. kn.	,, 50, 212
12 Cartomie Wood, Edderton	B/C1	co.	cr.	ci. in stone circle, d. 100	,, 7, 269
13 Old House of Assynt	0	0	M.	ci. cres.	Arch. Scot., 3, pl. V
14 Dalmore, Alness	B	hr.	M.	ci. in cemetery	Proc., 13, 257
15 Drummond, Kiltearn	B2a	hr,	sk.	ci. (one of two together)	,, 23, 138
16 Easter Moy, Urray	B1?	FR.	—	ci.u. cairn, scraper	,, 42, 66
17 Kilcoy	C3	hr.	?cr.	ci.? excentric in ca.	,, 43, 134
MORAY					
18 Burgie Lodge, Rafford	0	0	M.	ci. ⎫	
19 ,, ,, ,,	0	0	sk.	ci. cres. ⎬ small cemetery	,, 50, 238
20 ,, ,, ,,	0	0	sk.	ci. cres. ⎭	
21 ,, ,, ,,	0	0	—	ci.	
22 Roseisle	0	0	sk	ci. cres.	,, 3, 46
23 Newmills, Alves	frag.	—	?	ci. cres.	,, 12, 299
24 Carsewell, ,,	—	—	—	ci. in Elgin Museum	
25 Branstone, Urquhart	0	0	sk.	ci. cres.	,, 2, 531

No.	Site	Type				Reference
26–7	Kenny's Hillock, ,,	?A	wh.	—	ci. in cairn, diam. 24 ft.	Proc., 14, 109
28	Sliepie's H., Urquhart	Bfh.	—	—	ci.	Abercromby, 421
29	L. of Blairs, Altyre	C1	st.	cr.	ci.	Proc., 66, 404
30	Pluscarden	o	o	—	ci.	
31	Cawdor	B	wh.	—	ci. barrel-shaped beads	NMA
	NORTH-EAST SCOTLAND					
32	Gask, Turriff	?B2	mg.	—	— in cairn	Proc., 22, 331
33	Netherdale	B1a	hr.	—	—	
34	Fordyce	?C3	—	—	— in Banff Mus.	
35	Muthill, Peterhead	A	stamp	cr.	ci.	,, 22,381
36	Manse, Rosemarkie	B1a	hr.	sk.	ci.	,, 38,469
37	Methlick	A	FR	?	ci. under cairn	,, 1, 137
38	Sunnyside, Fyvie	B	—	—	— in bare earth	,, 63,367
39	Blackhill, ,,	B	—	M.	ci. under oxhide	
40	Wartle, Rayne	A	wh.	—	—	,, 24, 10
41	Pitcaple Castle	—	—	—	—	,, 59,210
42	Blinmill, Rothienorman	Bfh.	mg.	—	ci. under cairn, cres. amber	,, 6, 203
43	Tillybin, Kintore	B1	hr.	—	ci.	,, 2, 219
44	Boghead, ,,	o	o	?.	?. cres.	,, 12, 294
45	Haddo House estates	B1a	mg.	—	—	,, 60, 99
46	,, ,,	B1b	co.	—	—	,, 60, 99
47	Cairn Curr, Alford	Bfh.	co.	cr.	ci. excentric u. ca., cres.	
48	Migvie, Tarland	?B	mg.	cr.	ci. cairn	
49	Clashfaquhar, Banchory	?	?.	sk.	ci. with Beaker 23	,, 22, 363

FR., false-relief; co., cord ornament; hr., herring-bone; mg., maggot; wh., whipped cord; st., stab; sk., skeleton; M., male; F., female; DFV., Diminished Food Vessel; cr., cremation; ci., cist; ca., cairn; cres., crescentic jet necklace.

	TAY TO MOUNTH	Type	Ornament	Burial Rite	Associations	
50	Stonehaven	?C	hr.	—	—		Proc., 70, 357
51	„	Bfh.	—	—	?.		„ 50, 212
52	Fordoun	o	o	ci.	cres.		„ 17, 449
53	Kinneff	C2	FR.	sk.	—	2 bz. armlets and ?dagger	„ 6, 88
54	Bogheadly, Fettercairn	?C.U.	—	—	—	cres.	„ 22, 403
55	Craigneston, „	—	—	—	—		
56	Milton H., Tarfside	Bfh.	—	sk.	ci.		
57	Den o' Leuchland, Brechin	C2	fr.	—	ci.	cres. slug knife	„ 68, 412
58	Flawcraig, Kinnaird	B1b	hr.	sk.	ci.		„ 49, 16
59	Deerpark, „	B1a	hr.	—	ci.		„ 30, 201
60–2	„ „	o	o	—	cists		„ 30, 201
63	Pitkennedy, Aberlemno	o	o	sk.	ci.		„ 3, 78
64	Pitreuchy, Forfar	B1	—	sk.	ci.		„ 41, 65
65	Lunan Head, „	B	hr.	sk.	ci.	2 cres.	„ 12, 288
66	Sandiford, Kirriemuir	o	o	—	ci.	cres. (another cist & Beaker near)	
67	„ „	B2a	hr.	—	ci.		„ 70, 352
68	Meikle Kenny, Kingoldrum	Bfh.	—	—	—		N.M.A., E.E. 17
69	Meigle	Co	—	—	—		Proc., 73, 331
70	Mill of Queich, Alyth	B1b	hr.	—	ci.		
71	Newton Farm, Cupar	?B	—	—	ci.	at Hallyburton Ho.	
72	Knockenny, Glamis	frag.	—	sk.	ci.	jet beads	„ 65, 419
73	Murley Well, „	B1a	co..	—	ci.		„ 5, 81
74	Balkalk, Tealing	B	—	sk.	ci.	cres., bz. pin, fl. kn.	„ 14, 260
75	„ „	o	o	sk.	ci.	one of several	„ 14, 262
76	Hatton Cairn, Inverarity	?A	—	—	ci.	excentric u. cairn	„ 24, 12

No.	Site					Notes	Reference
77	Zabothy Hillock, „	Bob	—	—	ci.		„ 24, 9
78	„ „ „	Bfh.	st.	—	ci.		
78b	Gallows Hill, Kirkbuddo	B1b	—	—	ci.		acquired N.M.A. 1944
79	Letham Grange, Arbroath	Bfh.	—	—	ci.		*Proc.*, 5, 122
80	„ „	o	—	—	ci.	under ca. diam. 52 ft.	
81	Skichen, Carmyllie	B1a	hr.	—	ci. „ „ „	inverted, very small	„ 32, 239
82	„	?A	wh.	cr.	—		„ 6, 313
83	Camus Cross, Monikie	B	hr.	sk.	ci.	gold pommel mount	„ 2, 447
84	Carr Hill, „	Bfh.	co.	—	ci.		„ 6, 313
85	Kellas, Murroes	B1	—	—	ci.	disc bead	„ 24, 9
86	Barnhill, Broughty Ferry	B1	FR.	—	ci.	just outside edge	„ 21, 320
87	„ „ „	o	o	—	ci.	bz. dag. Au disc } under cairn	
88	„ „ „	o	o	—	ci.	bz. dag.	„ 21, 320
89–90	„ „ „	o	o	—	cis.		
91	Stannergate, Dundee	?A	?FR.	—	ci.	overlying meso.	„ 13, 303
92–4	„ „	o	o	—	cis.	midden	„ 13, 303
95	Greenford, Panmure	?A	FR.	cr.	ci.		„ 1, 86
96–8	Sherifftown, Perth	B2	wh.	cr.	in pits		„ 52, 133
92a	Ninewells, Invergowrie	B	co.	—	—		N.M.A., E.E. 40
	UPPER TAY AND FORTH BASINS						
99	Balnaguard, Grandtully	?	?	?	ci.	near standing stone	„ 42, 138
100	Craigie, Little Dunkeld	B1a	hr.	sk.	ci.	2 vases ?together	„ 19, 333
101	Moulin	B1b	—	—	—		„ 12, 90
102	Bruach, Glenlyon	C2	FR.	sk.	ci.	(headless skel., M.	„ 19, 39
103	Glenalmond	B1	hr.	—	—		
104	Broich, Crieff	B1	st.	?cr.	ci.	cairn	

No.	Site	Type	Ornament	Burial Rite	Associations
	UPPER TAY AND FORTH BASINS				
105	Dunblane	—	—	sk.; ci., dagger	T.S.A.S., i, 28
106	Keir, Dunblane	B1b	—	cr.; ci.	
107	Station, Doune	unclassed	wh. st.	—	Proc., 36, 685
108	Glenhead, „	Bfh.	mg.	ci., cairn, mace	„ 17, 452
	WEST HIGHLANDS				
109	Kishorn, Strathcarron	B/C	hr.	—	Inverness Mus.
110	Skye	C2	FR.	—	Hunterian Mus.
110a	Ardochy, Invergarry	Bfh.	—	ci.	N.M.A., E.E. 39
111	Quinish, Mull	Bfh.	—	ci.	Proc., 27, 369
112	Ardachy, Bunessan, Mull	B1	hr.	sk.; ci., several cists	„ 31, 116
113	„ „	B	?	sk.; ci.	
114–16	Uragaig, Colonsay	?	—	sks.; cis.	
117	Dunstaffnage, Lorne	A	—	sk.; ci.	„ 11, 468
117a	Benderloch village	B	—	—	„ 67, 326
118	Oban	C2	o	sk.; ci.	„ 56, 365
119	Melfort	o	o	ci., cres. bz. armlet	„ 19, 134
120	„	o	o	ci.	
121	Craignish	B1	co.	sk.; ci.	
122	„	Bfh.	hr.	sk.; ci., stone axe	„ 70, 397
123	„	o	o	sk.; ci.	
124	Staterach, Kerrera	Bfh.	—	ci.	„ 66, 406
125	„ „	C2	wh.	ci.	
126	L. Awe, lower end	B2b	FR.	ci.	„ 20, 74

FIRTH OF CLYDE PROVINCE

No.	Site	Type				Description	Reference
127	Carnasserie, Kilmartin	C2	hr.	—	ci.	cairn, diam. 50 ft.	,, 65, 275
128	Kilmartin Glebe	A1a	FR.	—	ci.	at centre of circle d. 27 ft., cres. } under cairn	,, 6,340 and
129	,, ,,	C2	—	cr.	ci.	long cist, cres. } d. 11 110 ft.	,, 39, 232
130	Poltalloch	o	o		gr. ci.	cres. ochre	
131	,,	C2	FR.		gr. ci.	ochre	,, 63, 162
132	Duncrachaig, Kilmartin	A	—	cr.	ci.	skels. on capstone and under floor } under cairn	Proc., 6,347
133	Rudhil	A	FR.	—	ci.	excentric } d. 100	,, 39, 235
134	,,	Bfh	—		ci.	under cairn	,, 6, 350
135–6	,,	o	o		cis.	diam. 90 ft. slug.	,, 39, 239
137	Barsloisnach	A	FR.		ci.		,, 39, 239
138	Balnabraid, Campbeltown	B1	—	cr.	ci.	secondaries in long chambered cairn No. 315	,, 54, 172
139	,, ,,	?C2	—	cr.	ci.		
140	,, ,,	?A	—	infant	ci.		
141	,, ,,	A	—		—		
142	Ascog, Cowal	—	—	?cr.	ci.		
143	,, ,,	o	—	?cr.	ci.		
144	Kilmichael, Bute	fr.	—	—	ci.		
145	Craigmore, ,,	fr.	plain		ci.	u. cairn, cres., bz. pin	T.B.N.H., 1930, 55
146	Mt. Stuart, ,,	C2	hr.	F.	ci.	diam. 45 ft., bead	,, Proc., 38, 63
147	Scalpsie Bay, ,,	B1b	FR.		ci.	,, bz. ?pin	,, 38, 52
148	Kilmory, ,,	B1	—	child	ci.		,, 68, 425
149–50	,, ,,	o	o	,,	cis.		
151	Brownhead, Arran	C2	hr./FR.	—	ci.	cairn, disc bead	,, 36, 120
152	Glenkill, ,,	B1a	—	sk.	ci.		,, 21, 161

No.	Location	Type	Ornament	Burial Rite	Associations	References
FIRTH OF CLYDE PROVINCE						
153	Mauchrie Moor II, Arran	C2	FR.	—	ci. in circle d. 45 ft. 4 in. a. hs.	*Proc.*, 4, 506
154	„ IV „	C2	FR.	cr.	ci. „ d. 27, bz. pin, a.h.	
155	„ III „	B	—	—	ci. „ 2 a. hs.	
156	„ „ „	B	—	sk.	ci.	
157	Clachaig, Arran	?C2	hr.	sk.	ci. secondary in c.c.	„ 36, 91
158	„ (Flagstaff), Arran	?C2	hr.	—	ci.	
159	Knockankelly, „	B1	hr.	sk.	ci.	„ 20, 170
160	Whitehouse, „	B1	—	sk.	ci.	
161	White Bay, Cumbrae	?	—	cr.	ci.	
162	„ „	o	o	sk.	ci.	*T.G.A.*, ii, 115
163	„ „	B	co.	cr.	ci.	
164	„ „	B1b	hr.	cr.	ci.	
165	Tomont End, „	B1a	FR.	cr.	ci. cairn, diam. 23 ft.	*T.G.A.*, ii, 117
166	„ „	A	FR.	cr.	ci. „ 21 ft.	„ ii, 117
167	Finnart Hill, L. Ryan	A	FR.	—	ci. „ 25 ft.	*Proc.*, 78, 136
CLYDE VALLEY						
168	Old Kilpatrick	B1	co.	sk.	ci.	
169	Knappers, Kilbowie, Glasgow	B	hr.	cr.	— from cremation cemetery, com-	*Proc.*, 69, 352
170	„ „	?B	—	?cr.	— prising some 33 deposits,	to
171	„ „	B1a	hr.	—	ci. including bz. dag., seg. paste	382
172	„ „	frag.	hr.	?cr.	— beads, jet beads, flint adze	
173	„ „	B1	—	?cr.	—	
174	„ „	o	o	cr.	ci. a.h.	
175	Mount Vernon, Glasgow	B1	—	sk.	ci. 'oats and rye'	Kelvingrove Museum, Glasgow
176	„ „	o	o	sk.	ci.	

No.	Place	Type				Notes	Reference
177	,, ,,	C	—	F.	ci.		
178	,, ,, ,,	o	o	sk.	ci.		
179	Baillieston, Glasgow	B		cr.	—	bare earth	
180	,, ,,	C2		cr.	—	,, ,,	T.G.A., ix, 288
181	,, ,,	o		cr.	—	,, ,,	
182	Blantyre, Coatshill	B1		—	—		
183	Blochairn, Baldernoch	?	FR.	—	—	on slab, bz. ?a.h.	
184	Drumsargard, Cambuslang	B1	FR.	—	—		,, i, 306
185	Dechmount Hill, ,,	Bfh.	co.	—	—		,, i, 229
186	Newton, ,,	B1	—	—	—	small cairn	Proc., 17, 381
187	Dalton, ,,	C3	FR.	cr.	ci.		,, 16, 147
188	Cathkin Moor, East Kilbride	B1	hr.	—	—		Wilson, History of Cambuslang
189	Drumpellier, Coatbridge	C4	—	—	—		Glasgow Herald, November 11, 1930
190	Dalserf, Hamilton	B2	co.	—	—		Ure, Kilbride and Rutherglen, 215
191	,, ,,	C2	FR.	sk.	—		
192	,, ,,	?	hr.	—	—		Abercromby, 261
193	Stonehouse, Hamilton	A	wh.	—	—	under tiny cairn	,, 262
194	F.-C. Canal, Cadder	B1	hr.	cr.	ci.		Hunterian Mus.
195	Knocken, Lesmahagow	C6	hr.	cr.	ci.	in cemetery, comprising in	Proc., 62, 230
196	,, ,,	B	—	cr.	ci.	all 16 small cists	T.G.A., iii, 500
197	,, ,,	C4	hr.	cr.	cis.		
198–9	,, ,,	o	o	cr.			
200	FIFE, KINROSS, ETC. Harvieston, Dollar	B	hr.	sk.	ci.	with cupmarked cap. in circle, diam. 60 ft.	Proc., 29, 195
201	Cumingar, Tillicoultry	B1a	hr.	—	ci.		
201a	,,	B	co.	—	—		,, 48, 337

		Type	Ornament	Burial Rite	Associations	Proc.
	FIFE, KINROSS, ETC.					
2202	Battle Law, Naughton	B1b	wh.	cr.	ci. cairn, diam. 50 ft.	Proc., 35, 301
2203	„ „	B1	hr.	—	ci. „	
2204	Greenhill, Balmerino	B1	hr.	cr.	—	„; 36, 635
2205	„ „	DFV	—	—	⎱ under cairn, diam. 50 ft.,	
2206	„ „	B	—	cr.	⎰ with empty centracil.	
2207	„ „	AB	mg.	cr.	Loose disc beads	
2208	„ „	B2	—	cr.		
2209	„ „	C	hr.	cr.		
2210	Beley, Dunino	B1a	mg.	sk.	ci.	„ 60, 21
2211	Rumgally, Cupar	C1	wh.	sk.	ci. slug	„ 66, 68
2212	„ „	o	o	sk.		
2213	Burnside, Kettle	A	FR.	—		
2214	Balgay, Newport	B1b	—	—	ci. cres.	
2215	Pitmillie, St. Andrews	?	mg.	sk.	ci.	„ 7, 255
2216	Kingsbarns Law, Crail	B1a	wh.	sk.	ci.	„ 10, 244
2217	„ „	B1	hr.	sk.		
2218	Craighead, „	B1a	co.	F.	ci. sheep bone	„ 48, 12
2219	Elie	?	hr.	—	other 'urns' too	
2220	Pitreavie, Dunfermline	B	wh.	sk.	ci.	„ 20, 240
2221	„ „	B1	—	sk.	ci.	
2222	„ „	C	—	sk.	ci.	
2223	„ „	?	—	sk.	ci.	
2224	Calais Moor, „	Ba	hr.	—	ci. cairn, diam. 40 ft.	„ 20, 247
2225	Harelaw Cairn	C2	FR.	cr.	ci. secondaries in cairn,	„ 25, 70
2226	„ „	B1a	hr.	cr.	ci. diam. 35 ft.	„ 26, 115
2227	Braehead, Kirkcaldy	?	mg.	—	ci.	Kirkcaldy Museum

No.							Reference
227a	Tulliallan	B	—	—			Proc., 69, 119
	LOTHIANS AND FORTH:						
228	Birkhill, Cambusbarron	B2b	FR.	—	ci.		Proc., 3, 245
229	„	C3	hr.	—	†	? mace and flint kn.	„ 21, 265
230	„	Bfh.	wh.	F.	—		„ 57, 245
231	Camelon, Falkirk	B	co.	—	ci.		
232		o	o	cr.	ci.		
233	Cowdenhill, Bowness	B	FR.	sk.	ci.		„ 40, 317
234	Bridgeness	B	—	M.	ci.		
235	„	Bfh.	st.		ci.		„ 58, 290
236	„	B	hr.	sk.			
237	Ratho	B1b	FR.	—	—	with bz. armlet (lost)	
238	Juniper Green	Bfh.	—	cr. inverted	ci.	C.U. and cist close by	„ 33, 354
239	„	B1b	—	cr.	„		
240	Beechwood Mains, Corstorphine	B1b	hr.	—	ci.		„ 4, 379
241	N. Gyle, Corstorphine	B1	FR.	—	ci.		„ 63, 368
242	Cramond	B	st.	—	—		
243	Marchwell, Glencorse	frag.	—	—	—	from ruined stone circles	
244	Succoth Pl., Edinburgh	B	mg.	—	—		„ 75, 220
245	„	A1	FR.	—	ci.	in double cist	
246	N. Merchiston cem.	B	—	—	ci.		„ 36, 670
247	Oxgangs Rd., Edinburgh	C2	FR.	—	—	V-perforated button	Proc., 68, 351
248	Shiel Loch, Torcraik	B	FR.	—	—		
249	Costerton Mains, Blackshiel	C2	co.	—	ci.		
250	Borthwick	B1a	—	—	—		„ 69, 13
251	Dobbies Knowe	Bfh.	—	—	—		

		Type	Ornament	Burial Rite	Associations
LOTHIANS AND FORTH					
252	Inveresk	?A	co.	—	ci.	Proc., 72, 135
253	Wardie, Newhaven	Bfh.	—	—	ci.	Arch. Scot., iv, 302
254	Bellefield, Musselburgh	B	wh.	sk.	ci.	Proc., 32, 8
255	Winton Park, Cockenzie	B1b	co.	cr.	ci. (small)	,, 66, 403
256	Gala Law, Luffness	Bfh.	—	—	ci.	B.N.C., x, 306
257	Kilspindie, Aberlady	Bfh.	—	—	ci.	Proc., 64, 193
258	,,	o	o	F.	—	
259	Longniddry	?A	st.	—	—	
260	Gullane Links	B1	co.	—	—	B.N.C., x, 306
261	Ormiston	?	hr.	—	—	
262	Duncra Hill, Pencaitland	B } B A }	—	sk.	ci.	Proc., 34, 131
263	Humbie Mill, Humbie	Bfh.	—	—	ci.	,, 7, 198
264	West Links, N. Berwick	Bfh.	—	F.	ci. ? in midden	
265	Knockenbaid, Dunbar	?C	hr.	—	ci.	
266	Near Dunbar	B1	FR.	—	—	
267	Skateraw, Innerwick	Bfh.	—	sk.	ci.	,, 74, 141
TWEED BASIN					
268	Earnsheugh, Coldingham	Bfh.	—	—	ci.	,, 28, 58
269	Cockburn Mill, St. Bathans	B1a	hr.	—	ci.	,, 46, 244
270	Broomhill, Duns	—	—	sk.	ci.	B.N.C., xxiv, 184
271	Houndwood Lye, Reston	—	—	sk.	ci.	,, ix, 15, 56
272	Aycliffe House, Ayton	B1b	—	sk.	ci.	,, vii, 274
273	,,	o	o	sk.	ci. (12 cists in all)	,,

No.	Place					Notes	Reference
274	Eddington Mill, Chirnside	B1b	co.	sk.	ci.	cairn with Beaker	Proc., 48, 330
275	Hagg Wood, Foulden	B	hr.	cr.	ci.	cairn, diam. 31 ft. under it,	,, 48, 318
276	,, ,, ,,	C2	co.	cr.	ci.	'also battle-axe	
277	High Cocklaw, Berwick	B	—	—	ci.	cres., flint knife	,, 63, 370
278–80	,, ,, ,,	o	o	—	cis.		
281	Cadger's Cairn, Gordon	B2	—	—	—	cairn	B.N.C., x, 115
282	Lintmill, Greenlaw	—	—	sk.	ci.		,, vii, 220
283	Halliburton, ,,	B1b	co.	—	ci.	? cairn	
284	Longcroft, Lauderdale	—	—	—	ci.	cairn, C.U. near by	Proc., 37, 32
285	Hillhouse, ,,	—	—	—	—		B.N.C., xxiv, 177
286	Blyth, ,,	—	—	—	ci.		
287	Heiton Mill, Kelso	Ba	FR.	sk.	ci.		Proc., 67, 165
288	Otterburn, Morebattle	B1	hr.	?cr.	ci.		B.N.C., xi, 177
289	Galashiels	B1	hr.	—	—		,, xi, 487
290	Linton Mains, Jedburgh	Bfh.	—	sk.	ci.		,, vi, 347
291	Crailing Hall, Jedburgh	Ba	hr.	—	ci.		Proc., 20, 100
292	Yetholm	B	co.	—	ci.		,, 17, 381
293	Darnhall, Eddleston	?	—	—	ci.		,, 10, 43
294–5	,, ,,	o	o	—	cis.		
296	,, ,,	Bfh.	—	—	ci.		
297	Rachan, Biggar	C2	—	—	—		,, 64, 25
	AYRSHIRE						
298	Wetherhill, Muirkirk	B1	—	cr.	—	cairn	,, 51, 25
299	Coilsfield, Tarbolton	—	—	cr.	ci.	carved capstone	App. to ,, 6, 27
300	Law, ,,	B	co.	—	—		
301	Content, St. Quenox	Bo	hr.	—	—		

		Type	Ornament	Burial Rite		Associations
	AYRSHIRE					
302	Townhead, Stevenston	?	—	sk.	ci. strike a light	Cat. Glasgow Exhib.
303	,, ,,	B1	—	sk.	ci.	
304	Waterworks, Ardrossan	B1	—	sk.	ci.	Thurnam, Crania Brit.
305	Kirkhill, ,,	Bfh.	co.	cr.	—	Proc., 5, 110
306	Wallacetown	B1b	hr.	—	—	,, 26, 58
307	Skelton	Bb	hr.	—	—	A.C.A., i, 247
308	Maybole	B1/C2 FR.	FR.	—	—	,, i, 49
	GALLOWAY					
309	Cairngaan, Kirkmaiden	B(E)	—	sk. oval grave		,, v, 44
310	Port Spittal, Portpatrick	B1	co.	sk.	ci.	Cat. Glasgow Exhib., 828
311	Craigbirnoch, New Luce	B1	FR.	cr.	ci. cairn, diam. 37 ft.	Proc., 51, 26
312	Stairhaven	—	—	cr.	— cairn	,, 55, 53
313	Craigenhollie, Old Luce	—	FR.	sk.	—	,, 14, 142
314	Lochinch, Inch	C2	—	cr.	— disc beads	,, 21, 189
315	Stoneykirk	Bfh.	—	—	ci.	,, 36, 585
316	Blairbuie, Glasserton	Bfh.	mg.	—	ci. primary under cairn, diam. 46 ft.	
317	Drannandow, Minnigaff	B1	hr.	—	ci. excentric	,, 57, 63
318	,, ,,	C3	hr.	—	— in round cist, cairn d. 65 ft.	
319	High Banks, Kirkcudbright	C4	FR.	cr.	— excentric in cairn, d. 65 ft.	,, 25, 25
320	,, ,,	B	o	—	—	,, 25, 27
321	Glenarm, Urr	B2	hr.	—	—	
322	Kirkmabreck	B	hr.	—	—	
323	Closeburn, Dumfries	Bfh.	co.	sk.	— flints	Arch. Scot., iii

V. EXTENDED BURIALS OF STAGE IV

(i) At Bishopsmill, near Elgin, a boat-shaped cist, 6 ft. long, 3 ft. wide at the centre, but tapering to 1 ft. at each end, contained a halberd blade and an oxhide that had presumably covered an extended skeleton (Stuart, *Sculptured Stones of Scotland*, ii (1867), p. xcvi.)

(ii) On Craigscorrie farm, near Beauly, an oval cist, 7 ft. long by 4 ft. wide and cut to a depth of 2 ft. into the solid rock, contained an extended skeleton, accompanied by a stout blade with a wide mid-rib and wide grooves on either side (? a halberd), two tanged and barbed arrow-heads and a flint knife, the grave-goods having all been exposed to the action of fire (*Proc.*, lix, 205; lxxviii, 138).

(iii) At Stittenham, in the Alness valley, a huge cairn 108 ft. in diameter and 20 ft. high, when removed in 1826, was found to cover a shaft grave 12 ft. by 7 ft. 9 in. by 8 ft., which contained a cist walled with seven upright slabs and measuring 8 ft. by 2 ft. 6 in. by 2 ft. It contained no bones, but many fragments of carbonized oak, a shale disk 2 in. in diameter, and three tanged and barbed arrow-heads with serrated edges (*T.G.S.I.*, xii (1886), 333; *Proc.*, lxvi, 18).

(iv) On Kilmartin glebe a cairn 110 ft. in diameter covered a central shaft grave 7 ft. 6 in. by 3 ft. by 3 ft., lined with boulders in which no bones were found (presumably, therefore, a decayed skeleton), but Food Vessel 124 of type C2 and a crescentic necklace (*Proc.*, vi, 340).

(v) The primary cist under a composite cairn at Gilchorn (Arbroath) exposed in 1810 was 5 ft. long, stood in a shaft 6 ft. by 3 ft. by 3 ft.; on re-excavation in 1891, a grooved dagger over $3\frac{1}{2}$ in. long and another tapering blade with a rounded midrib $5\frac{1}{4}$ in. long and $1\frac{1}{2}$ in. wide were found in the shaft. Secondary interments in Cinerary Urns assign this grave to stage IV (*Proc.*, xxv, 447).

(vi) At Ri Cruin, Kilmartin, the southernmost of three cists in a ruined cairn, is 6 ft. 5 in. long, 3 ft. 4 in. to 2 ft. 2 in. wide, and 2 ft. 9 in. deep; two of the side slabs are covered with representations of flat axes.

(vii–viii) Burials in oak-tree coffins from Cairngill, Longside, Aberdeenshire (*N.S.A.*, xii, 354), and from a cairn on Dumglow on the Fife-Kinross border (*Proc.*, xxxix, 179) should, on English analogies, belong to the Food-Vessel complex.

(ix) Though no dimensions are available, the burial in a cist covered by capstone measuring 9 ft. by 5 ft. by 3 ft. under 'an immense cairn' at Skateraw, East Lothian, sounds as if it should belong here; it contained a bronze knife-dagger with a gold-mounted pommel (*Proc.*, xxvii, 7).

(x) A cairn, 50 ft. in diameter, at Barnhill, near Dundee, is said to
      have covered a central 'long cist' built above ground and peri-
      pheral short cists, one containing a knife-dagger (*Proc.*, xxi, 321).

The similarity of the foregoing burials to English graves of my
Period IV is obvious. Two other rich burials may be mentioned in
the same context on the strength of the typology of the daggers they
contain.

(xi) At Blackwater Foot, Arran, a huge cairn covered a cist, only
      4 ft. 3 in. by 2 ft. 4 in. by 2 ft. 6 in., that contained, presumably
      with a totally decayed skeleton, a dagger (Fig. 13) 9¼ in. long,
      strengthened with three convergent ribs on each face, with a gold
      hilt-mount similar to those from Balmerino, Monikie, and
      Skateraw.

(xii) On a peak of the Sidlaws above Wester Mains of Auchterhouse,
      a composite cairn, 62 ft. in diameter, covered a double cist with
      a total internal length of 4 ft., containing two cremations unurned,
      one accompanied by a dagger 7 in. long with a triple midrib and
      a hilt of ox-horn (*Proc.*, xxxii, 211).

VI. DAGGER GRAVES

(A) FLAT, ROUND-HEELED DAGGERS

1	Cairn Greg, Linlathen Angus	5″×2″	sk.	ci.	under large cairn with (late) Beaker, 125	*Proc.*, 6, 98
2	Callachally, Glenforsa, Mull	frags.	—	ci.	with Beaker 198 and wrist-guard	,, 9, 537
3	Kirkcaldy, Fife	$4\frac{1}{2}$″×$1\frac{1}{2}$″	sk.	ci.	juxtaposed to cist containing Beaker 202a	,, 78, 112
4	Collessie, Fife	6″×$2\frac{1}{4}$″ with ribbed gold pommel-mount	cr.	—	under same cairn as graves containing Beakers 199, 200, but nearer the periphery than either	,, 12, 439
5	Doune Rd., Dunblane	$4\frac{3}{8}$″×1″	sk.	ci.	with Food Vessel 105	*T.S.A.S.*, i, 28
6	Camus Cross, Monikie, Angus	ribbed gold pommel-mount	sk.	ci.	with Food Vessel 83	*Proc.*, 2, 447
7	Barnhill, Broughty Ferry	$3\frac{7}{8}$″	sk.	ci.	with 2 gold discs in Food Vessel	,, 21, 320
8	,, ,, ,,	lost			cemetery	
9	Knappers, Kilbowie	$4\frac{1}{4}$″×$1\frac{1}{2}$″	—	—	in cremation cemetery in which were also Food Vessels 169–74	,, 69, 355
10	Letham Quarry, Perth	$3\frac{1}{8}$″	sk.	ci.		,, 31, 184
11	Drumlanrich, Callander	$4\frac{1}{2}$″×$1\frac{3}{4}$″	—	ci.		,, 12, 456
12	Cleish, Loch Nell	5″×$2\frac{1}{4}$″	—	ci.	under large cairn	,, 10, 84
13	Skateraw, Dunbar	$5\frac{7}{8}$″ with ribbed gold pommel-mount	—	ci.	under huge cairn	,, 27, 7
14	Carlochan Cairn, Chapelerne, Crossmichael, Kirkcudbright	$4\frac{3}{4}$″	—	—	under cairn	,, 12, 456

						N.M.A.
15	Dunragit Station, Wigtons	3¾"	—	—	in gravel pit	—

(B) MIDRIB AND GROOVED (OGIVAL) DAGGERS

						N.M.A.
(a)	Gilchorn, Arbroath	over 3½" with lateral grooves over 5½" with flat round midrib	—	—	in shaft under centre of large cairn	Proc., 25, 447
(b)	Westermains of Auchterhouse, Angus	7" 1·9 rivets, triple midrib	cr.	ci.	under large cairn	„ 32, 211
(c)	Blackwater Foot	9¼" 3 convergent ribs, ribbed gold pommel-mount	sk.	ci.	cairn	„ 36, 118
(d)	Law of Maudslie, Carluke, Lan.	5¾" with midrib	sk.	ci.		„ 12, 454

Note that the gold pommel-mounts of Nos. 4, 6, 13, and (c) (Figs. 12, 13) are identical. Another was found with a grooved dagger and a Food Vessel in Eire.

VII. THE TYPOLOGY OF BRONZES

The metal weapons, tools, and ornaments found in graves and hoards, owing to their orderly development, can be divided into typological groups that probably succeed one another in time despite overlaps. The main groups, frequently associated together, are:

Early Bronze Age 1: flat axes and flat round-heeled knife-daggers.

Early Bronze Age 2: flanged axes, grooved and midrib daggers, and tanged spear-heads.

Middle Bronze Age: palstavs, rapiers, socketed spear-heads with loop on sockets.

Late Bronze Age: socketed axes, swords, socketed spear-heads with peg-holes in the socket, razors, etc.

Types of E.B.A.2 are found in graves of the Wessex culture in England, so are crescentic necklaces of amber otherwise similar to those found with Food Vessels in Scotland. Hence the types of E.B.A.2, as well as those of 1, should belong to stage IV. But in North and Central Europe halberds imported from Ireland are as early as, or earlier than, British imports of Wessex type. So halberds in Scotland, too, should go back to stage IV (cf. *P.C.B.I.*, 164).

Types of M.B.A. are practically unknown in Scotland north of the Southern Uplands. Even south of that range a rapier and palstav were associated in a hoard from Glentrool, Galloway, with a spear-head, a razor, and a torque that are proper to L.B.A. (Childe, *P.C.B.I.*, 171; Hawkes, *P.P.S.*, viii, 38, n. 2), and a hoard is to be 'dated' by its latest constituents.

The L.B.A. in England is capable of subdivision into three complexes, of which the several types of sword are the most convenient indices: L.B.A.1, U-type swords; L.B.A.2, 'carp's tongue' swords; L.B.A.3, V-type swords. Only the latest type of sword is represented in Scotland, so that our L.B.A. may begin only with L.B.A.3. As none of the distinctive bronze types has ever been found in a grave (for the funerary razors are unlike those found in the hoards), their attribution to stage V depends upon the absolute chronology of that stage as discussed in Appendix IX.

VIII. CINERARY URNS AND THEIR CONTENTS

The most important graves only out of my (admittedly incomplete) list of 665 need be reproduced here. The urns of the Overhanging Rim family are numbered according to their position in the theoretical degeneration series as traced in *Prehistoric Communities* beginning with I, the narrow-rimmed type unknown in Scotland. So II means an urn with broad overhanging rim, concave neck, and well-marked shoulder (Plate XI, 1); III, with heavy projecting rim, but flat neck and vague shoulder; IV, neckless urns (Figs. 14, 3, 5), either biconical, or (C) barrel-shaped with cordons in relief simulating the end of the rim and the shoulder (Cordoned Urns), and V, barrel-shaped vessels in which the surface is smooth, but a band of incised pattern generally marks the site of the once ornamented rim. ENC, Encrusted Urn; EFV, Enlarged, and DFV, Diminished, Food Vessels.

	ROSS		
22–7	Dalmore, Alness	ENC and ? in small cists in cemetery toggle	Proc., 13,255
28	Flowerburn Ho., Fortrose	frag. in small cist with strike a' light	,, 19, 352
29	Balnalick, Glenurquhart	plain ? EFV, razor, secondary in cairn	,, 22, 42
	MORAY		
32	Culbin Sands	C with strike a' light	,, 25, 504
	NORTH-EAST SCOTLAND		
40	Foulford, Cullen,	III	
41	,, Banffs.	EFV serrated a.h., bone pin	,, 31, 221
44	Down House, ,,	EFV, 13 a.hs, and bone pin	Pennant's Tour, i, pl. XXI
55	Strichen, Aberdeenshire	C with mace	Ant. J., vii, 518
72–5	Seggiecrook, Kennethmont	4 Cs, toggle, slate pend., clay beads	Proc., 42, 212
108	Knockolochie, Chapel of Garrioch	C under centre of cairn, diam. 40 ft.	,, 6, 276
110–6	Broomend of Crichie	EFV and bare crems., secondaries in fossed circle, mace	,, 35, 224
122–9	Tuack, Kintore	III, C f. 6 bare crs., in fossed circle	,, 35, 194
131	Tullochvenus, Tough	? razor, under cairn	Simpson, Province of Mar, 35
	TAY TO MOUNTH		
141	Mill of Marcus, Brechin	C, segmented bead	Proc., 24, 470
142–4	,, ,, ,,	EFV, 2 ?s, pigmy, cist	
157–8	Gilchorn, Arbroath	III, all secondaries in cairn	,, 25, 449
159–61	,,	3 ?s, 2 pigmies, bz. blade, paste bead	

FIFE

180–3	Westwood, Newport	3 IIIs } urns arranged in a circle	*Proc.*, 6, 388
184	„	C } barley?	
185–90	„	6 ?s	
191–9	Brackmont Mill, Leuchars	9 II's, toggle and ivory buckle	
200–3	„	4 III's	
204–5	„	2 ?s	„ 71, 252; 76, 84
206–8	„	3 bare cremations	
209	„	type E Food Vessel	
213–35	Carphin Ho., Creich	22 ?s, 14 in one row	„ 7, 405 and 13, 113
274–93	Law Park, St. Andrews	ENC, Cs, 2 razors	„ 41, 412
294–7	Kingskettle	2 III's, serrated a.h., pigmy	„ 55, 40
311	Calais Moor, Dunfermline	II, III, 4 Cs, 5 ?s, secondaries under cairn, F.V. primaries	„ 20, 246
328–31	Shanwell Ho., Milnathort	4 ? Cs, razor	„ 19, 114
332–3	„	2 bare cremations	„ 29, 190
334	Cuningar, Tillicoultry	III secondary in stone circle	Anderson, 63
336–55	Alloa	III and 19 ?s and cist with gold armlets on capstone	

LOTHIANS

356–8	Cambusbarron	3 IVs, stone mace	*Proc.*, 5, 213
464–6	Newbigging, Penicuik	3 ?s, razor, 'mound'	Gordon, *Itin. Septen.*, 110
475–81	Longniddry	5 IVs; ? EFV., quoit bead of paste	N.M.A.
482–5	Traprain Law	4 IIIs, pigmy	
487	Stobshield, Humbie	C, bz. blade $1\frac{3}{4}'' \times 1''$, with 2 rivet holes on line of greatest diam.	*Proc.*, 16, 473

AYRSHIRE

541	Wetherhill, Muirkirk	II under cairn	Proc., 51, 25
543	Marchhouse, ,,	III under cairn, bz. 'pin', bone pin	,, 61, 275
547–54	Nith Lodge, New Cumnock	2 pigmies, 6 crems., battle axe, in cairn	,, 72, 245
556–8	Beoch, ,, ,,	3 ?s secondaries in 'circle'	,, 72, 237
577–92	Ardeer, Stevenston	16 Vs in 'cemetery-cairn', star bead	,, 40, 378
593	Chapelton, Ardrossan	C, battle-axe	
612	Hunterston, W. Kilbride	C, jet disc bead	,, 62, 260
613–17	Largs	5 IIIs, mace	Archaeologia, 62, 245
		7 O.K. urns in one cist too	

WEST COAST

625	Oban	C, battle-axe	Proc., 32, 58

GALLOWAY

628	Sandmill, Stranraer	II, battle-axe, bronze blade, bone bead	,, 76, 80
632	Balneil, Glenluce	C, shouldered bz. chisel, bone crutch pin, paste quoit bead	,, 50, 303
634–5	Mid-Torrs, ,, :	2 IIs	,, 22, 67
649–58	Palmerston, Dumfries	3 ?s, riveted bz. blade, whetstone	A.C.A.W., vi, 87
		10 IVs in circle	T.D.G., 1931, 80
664	Shuttlefield, Lockerbie	?EFV, bz. blade, with midrib, 3″ long	Proc., 14, 281

CLYDE VALLEY

361	New Kilpatrick	?, serrated and leaf-shaped a. hs., bone toggle	,, 42, 218
363–5	Newlands, Glasgow	3 IIs	
366	,, ,,	EFV, 4 bare cremations	,, 39, 528

Notes on Grave Goods. The battle-axe found with the early urn, No. 628, would not be out of place in the English Wessex culture, while that accompanying Cordoned Urn 593 is a derivative developing towards the Bann type of Ireland, whereas blunting the edge would lead to the maces associated with Cordoned Urn 55 and cremation 111 in Aberdeenshire. Stray axes of the same 'waisted' forms turn up in Caithness and Orkney. The razors accompany urns of the late Cordoned type, if belonging to the Overhanging Rim series at all. The blade with 644 may possibly be a miniature sword, such as were sometimes deposited in Late Bronze Age graves in Denmark and Sicily.

Perforated toggles were contained in two early Overhanging Rim Urns (IIs), in one late Cordoned Urn, and in one Encrusted (22). Almost identical toggles are known from Late Bronze Age graves in Denmark. Segmented beads of an opaque vitreous material were contained in two very late urns (141, 577), and others were found in the cremation cemetery of the Knappers, Kilbowie, Glasgow, in which most but not all of the pottery belonged to the Food Vessel class. Quoit-shaped beads of a similar material come from the equally late urns, 475 and 632, and a star-shaped type from Nos. 64 and 577. Beck and Stone (*Arch.*, 85, 208, 233) admit that these Scottish beads differ both in form and material from unquestionably imported beads of 'Egyptian' fayence characteristic of the Wessex culture in England, and confess their 'total inability to find in any country specimens that are identical with the star, quoit, and Scottish segmented beads'. While the fashion, like so much else in the Urn culture, was certainly an heritage from the southern Wessex culture, its Scottish applications cannot be used as chronological guides nor accepted as imports from Egypt; Callander and Mann have suggested that they may have been made locally, and their thesis has not been disproved. Finally, an unique ivory buckle, found with an early stage II ORU at Brackmont Mill, while a faithful reproduction of a gold buckle from a rich Wessex barrow at Normanton, cannot be accepted as even probably synchronous with the Wiltshire object.

IX. ABSOLUTE CHRONOLOGY

The determination of the age in centuries before our era and the duration of the several successive stages, must begin from the known, i.e. the latest stage ending with the Roman invasion described in written history.

(1) *The broch culture.* Two lines of argument converge to prove that the broch culture as developed in the extreme North of Scotland must be substantially older than A.D. 80.

Firstly, the broch of Torwoodlee, near Galashiels (Fig. 18), one of the few emanations from the North Scottish focus in the Lowlands, yielded on excavation quite large quantities of imported Roman pottery of Flavian, i.e. first century, date. James Curle thought it unlikely that Agricola or his successors would have allowed a band of northern barbarians to establish themselves in the newly conquered province between A.D. 80 and 100. Even if they had, the tower was there by 100, and a substantial time must be allowed for the development of the parent culture in the north and the subsequent plantation of colonies in the Lowlands.

Secondy, so many elements of the northern broch culture, and in particular a whole series of textile appliances (Fig. 19) used by women are derived from the pre-Roman cultures of south-western England (especially the Glastonbury culture), that we must conclude that the broch-builders included a substantial contingent of immigrants of both sexes from south-western England. Now Hawkes has drawn my attention to a passage in Orosius (*Historiae adversum paganos*, VII, 6, 10), in which, after describing Claudius' annexation of Britain in 43, he adds, 'Orcadas etiam insulas ultra Britanniam in Oceano positas Romano adiecit imperio'. This statement may well just mean that the Orcadian chiefs sent envoys making formal submission; for that was a common move on the part of non-Belgic Gauls within Rome's sphere of influence. Hence the otherwise surprising reference to Orkney becomes quite intelligible on the assumption that the archipelago was dominated in 43 by a group—the broch-builders—who had recently arrived from some region on the Empire's fringe, southern England or western Gaul, where Roman alliances were habitually recognized as a move in inter-tribal politics. The latest probable occasion for such a migration would be the Belgic expansion into south-western England in the first half of the first century A.D.

(2) *The Gallic and vitrified forts*, containing brooches, pins, and axes more archaic than any found in brochs, and no Roman pottery whatsoever, must have been at least founded before the oldest known brochs. Where they occur, such forts constitute the earliest recognizable monuments of the Iron Age, i.e. stage VI. Hence the beginning of that stage round the Tay estuary, on Bute and in Morvern would also appear to be more or less dated by the perfectly correct assertion that the La Tène I (c) brooches (Fig. 2) from excavated monuments of the stage there, the Gallic forts of Abernethy, Dunagoil, and Rahoy, went out of fashion on the Continent about 250 B.C. But in reality, only if these forts had been built by invaders come direct from the Continent, would the La Tène brooches date them thus precisely; for Dr. Wheeler[1] has produced stratigraphical evidence and other convincing arguments to show that even in south-western England La Tène I (c) brooches might be worn even after 100 B.C. Now the assumption of a recent arrival is somewhat precarious. Ring-headed

[1] *Maiden Castle, Dorset*, p. 253.

pins, the other decisive indicators of an early date for these forts, are
a peculiarly British derivative of a continental Hallstatt form. And
they too, it is now known, had not gone out of fashion in England
altogether by 100 b.c.[1]

Furthermore, some Gallic forts including Dun Evan and Forgandenny itself are apparently bivallate. Now in England bivallate
defences are associated with Wheeler's sling complex[2] that is not likely
to have appeared there before, say, 150 b.c. Of course this argument
does not apply to outer ramparts that enclose an irregular outer bailey
below or around part of the inner enceinte; such outer baileys are
quite commonly attached to our Gallic forts and at Abernethy,
Duntroon, and probably also Finavon, their ramparts were built in
the same technique, and presumably at the same time, as the inner
defence. 'Bivallate', in this context at least, is applicable only to two
sets of parallel ramparts at no great distance apart. The outermost
might be a secondary addition, of course—only excavation can decide
—but at Forgandenny it seems an integral part of the whole work.
Hence, all we are so far entitled to assert is that some Gallic forts,
the earliest manifestations of stage VI in Scotland, may have been
founded between 350 and 50 b.c. Really, 100 is a more likely date
than 300 for the earliest documented remains of our last stage.

The end of *stage V* is not, however, thereby dated. There are
reported finds that could be interpreted as indications that the Late
Bronze Age equipment was still current after the use of iron had been
introduced in Gallic forts and that burials in Cinerary Urns may have
been taking place among some communities while others were living
in forts and even brochs. In the Roman camp of Ardoch a socketed
bronze axe was found under circumstances that convinced even Dr.
Anderson that it was a genuine instance of an overlap between the
Late Bronze and the Iron Ages.

A similar overlap between the funerary and domestic records might
be deduced from the following finds: at Edderton (Ross) a Cordoned
Urn was recovered from the fosse encircling a tumulus the primary
burial under which, a cremation in a cist, was accompanied by a blue
glass bead with white inlay not earlier than the La Tène period (*Proc.*,
v, 312). A 'jet' bracelet of La Tène type was found on the periphery
of the cairn at Drumelzier, into which had been inserted also six
Cordoned Urns (*Proc.*, lxv, 369 ff.). A bronze finger-ring of rather
later type was similarly situated on the edge of the Wardlaw cairn
near Muirkirk (*Proc.*, lvii, 13). In neither of these two cases is any
sort of association between the Iron Age objects and the urns established. In Queen Mary's Cairn, 18 ft. high and 120 ft. in diameter,
on the Cathkin Hills, East Kilbride, twenty-five urns, shown by Plate I,
to be of the Cordoned type, stood mouth down on the west side and
contained cremated bones, a two-edged 'comb' and a clasp of bronze

---

[1] *Maiden Castle, Dorset*, 269; cf. *Arch. J.*, xci, 269 ff.   [2] cf. *Antiquity*, xviii, 1944, p. 51.

and 'a ring of bituminous coal', 4 in. in diameter, 1 in. wide, and ¼ in. thick.[1] 'In the bottom of the cairn and exactly in the centre of the area it occupied was a coffin of large slabs, 4 ft. cube, with a gigantic coverstone. A little earth was all the treasure it contained, but close to it were many small bones, mostly in fragments, and among them two ornaments'—actually the terminal rings of a bridle-bit of a type not current before 50 B.C. The emptiness of the central cist implies that the primary burial had been disturbed, perhaps at the time the bit was deposited outside it. Theoretically, this deposit could have been made without disturbing the Urns concentrated on one side of the great cairn. Hence this old report does not prove the continuance of the burial practices distinctive of stage V, a couple of centuries after forts representative of stage VI had been built.

The 'fayence' beads having failed us (p. 128), the sole tenuous direct clue to the age of the poor interments in Cinerary Urns, distinctive of our stage V, is provided by the Danish analogies to the bone toggles. These Danish toggles belong to Montelius' typological period IV of the Northern Bronze Age and are very plausibly dated between 700 and 650 B.C.[2] They were in any case demonstrably contemporary with metal tools and weapons of the Late Bronze Age and afford some presumptive evidence that our Scottish ones were so too. In other words, that stage V comprises part of the Late Bronze Age in the metallurgical record. Now this 'Age' can to some extent be dated.

Admittedly all the Late Bronze Age objects from Scotland north of the southern Uplands are late (L.B.A.3) when judged by English standards, and even so might have arrived or at least persisted in this cultural backwater, long after they first emerged in England. The Huelva hoard—admitting that the assemblage of bronzes dredged up out of the harbour does constitute a closed find—would prove that spear-heads with lunate openings in the blade appropriate to this phase were being made in, and exported from, the British Isles by about 750 B.C. The application of this date to Scotland could only be justified by the discovery of some datable import in a Scottish hoard. Now the very typical and very remote Highland hoard of Adabrock, Lewis (Plate XII, 1), does contain such an object—part of a bronze cup. Mrs. Piggott ingeniously recognized this as one of a well-known group of cups[3] fashionable round the Alps in early Hallstatt times, before 600 B.C. Being an actual import, it is unlikely that it should have been included in a hoard even in the Hebrides more than a century later at the outside. In other words, stage V should have begun even in the Western Isles before 500 B.C. at latest.

A sort of limiting date for the closing phase of stage IV, reached again in a rather roundabout way, gives precision to the foregoing

[1] Ure, *History of Rutherglen and Kilbride* (Glasgow, 1793), 216–19, with plates I and V.
[2] Broholm, *Studier over den yngre Bronsalder*, 109, 250.
[3] Dechelette, *Manuel*, II, 2, p. 781; *Auh V*, I, xi, 1, 3; II, iii, V, 6; V, p. 404, n. 3; *M.Z.*, i (1906), p. 36.

suggestion. A grave in Holstein, at Gönnebek,[1] belonging to the previous typological period of the Northern Bronze Age, Montelius' III, contained a gold copy of, or casing for, a type A Food Vessel almost identical in form and ornamentation with that from Duncracaig, Kilmartin (132) (Plate VII, 1). But even before that (in Montelius' II) British spear-heads with basal loops had been imported into Holstein.[2] Now in Britain such spear-heads belong already typologically to our Late Bronze Age, albeit to its earlier phase represented in Scotland only by finds like the Glentrool hoard (Callander's Period III) from south of the Southern Uplands. This indirect evidence does not, of course, imply that socketed axes and slashing swords were used by our societies in stage IV; it does prove not only that the end of that stage falls chronologically within the Late Bronze Age of Britain as a whole, but also that type A Food Vessels come near the end rather than the beginning of the stage.

Its beginning could be more closely defined if we could assume that the Food Vessel culture of Scotland was partly synchronous, as well as systadial, with the Wessex culture of southern England. The assumption is reasonable; for one thing, crescentic necklaces that occur in Wessex graves are more likely to have been invented in Scotland than in England. Now many lines of argument converge to make it likely that the Wessex culture was flourishing between 1450 and 1350 B.C. and may go back even to 1600. If the halberds found in Scotland are correctly assigned to stage IV the higher date would apply here too. For some of them went on across Scotland to central and northern Europe, where they are assigned to Montelius' I and ought not to be much later than 1600 B.C.

This is the earliest likely historical date in Scottish prehistory. The favourite figure of 1800 B.C. for the Beaker invasion was devised for southern England and is at best a guess. Dates assigned to megalithic tombs depend upon undemonstrable typological theories and merely take the form of vague *termini post quos*.

X. THE BRONZE AGE IN SHETLAND AND ORKNEY

'NO bronze weapons, tools, nor ornaments have been recovered from any grave in Shetland and Orkney, and only four bronzes appropriate to stage III or IV (all from Orkney) are known.[3] But among the very numerous polished stone axes that continued in use in the isles long after they had been replaced by metal in the rest of Britain, are some with splayed blades imitating metal axes (Fig. 24) which must

---

[1] Kersten, *Zur älteren nordischen Bronzezeit*, pl. XXI.
[2] ibid., p. 65; cf. *M.Z.*, xxix (1934), p. 58.
[3] *Proc.*, xlii, 75; *R.C., Orkney*, p. 59 (3 daggers and one dirk).

accordingly have been known. The decorated plate from a crescentic jet necklace was found stray in a peat moss at Tankerness,[1] and another necklace of unknown type is reported to have been found in one of the cists of group A or B on the Links of Skail, while two gold discs and amber beads were found with a cremation in a full-sized

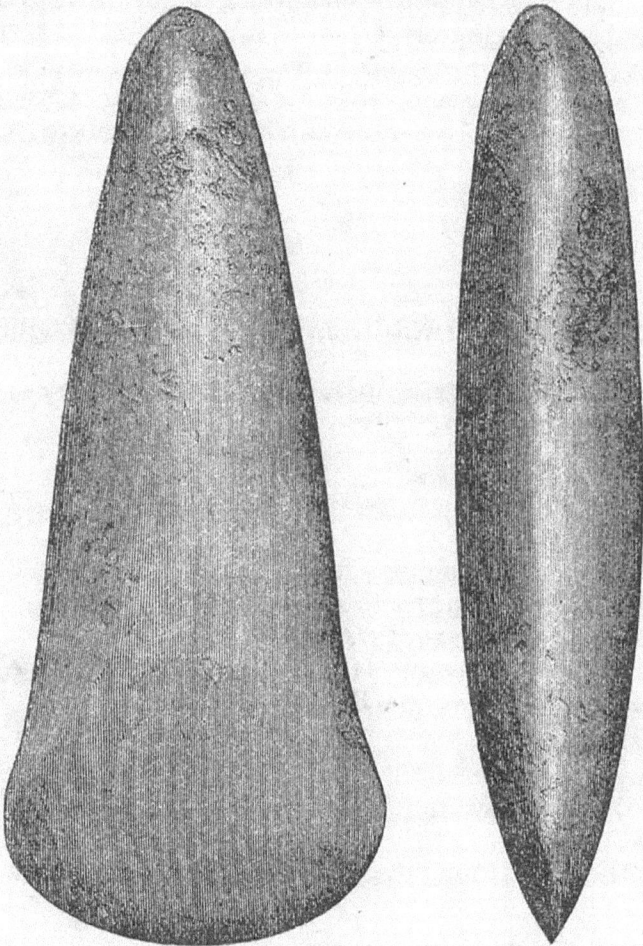

FIG. 24. STONE AXE IMITATING A BRONZE AXE, SHETLAND. ½

cist of group B under the largest of the Knowes of Trotty (Huntiscarth).[2] That by this time the Orcadian economy was already 'Bronze Age' in the sense of involving regular trade is, of course, proved by the use of steatite for funerary vessels since the material at least must have been brought from Shetland.

As in the rest of Scotland, the cists of groups A and B may be flat graves or surmounted by a large tumulus. Sometimes the same mound[3] covers several apparently contemporary cists like some cairns

[1] P.O.A.S., xiii, 41.   [2] Arch., xxxiv, 275.   [3] ibid., 107.

of stage IV in Fife. The larger urns, however, appear only in small tumuli comparable to the mainland small cairns or perhaps as secondaries in larger barrows.[1] As in Fife and Ross, we have cemeteries of flat graves sometimes comprising one full-sized cist and several smaller cists (like Plate VI, 3) or bare cremations.[2] The tumuli may often form cemeteries some comprising large and small barrows[3] others composed exclusively of small mounds like most Highland cairnfields. Multiple interments in the same cist, sometimes by both rites, are unusually common, while a number of cists of group B and a few of group C are two-storeyed[4] like the chambered cairns of Rousay and Eday.

XI. LIST OF GALLIC AND VITRIFIED FORTS

F., Face exposed on one side of rampart; FF., Faces exposed on both sides; G., Gallic fort showing beam sockets; V., vitrified.

MORAY FIRTH COASTS

1   Dun Creich, on Dornoch Firth, Sutherland, 170×95, R.C. *Sutherland*, No. 54
2   Knock Farril, Strathpeffer, Ross, 425×125–80, *T.I.S.S.*, vi, 290.
3   Dun Mor, Lovat Bridge, F, 205×90, *T.I.S.S.*, viii, 97.
4   Dun Fionn, Strathglass, *T.I.S.S.*, viii, 103
5   Ord of Kessock, at mouth of Beauly Firth, Ross, ? 800×150, ibid. 95.
6   Craig Phaidrig, Inverness, F, 250×90, ibid. 90.

GREAT GLEN

7   Dun Dearduil, Inverfarigaig, F, 105×80, ibid. 98.
8   Castle Urquhart.
9   Torr Duin, Fort Augustus, F, 70×30, *T.I.S.S.*, viii, 106.

MORAY FIRTH, SOUTH COASTS

10   Dun Daviot, Strath Nairn, 120×60.
11   Dun Evan, Cawdor, 200×75, *T.I.S.S.*, viii, 108.
12   Dunearn, Dulsie Bridge, on Findhorn, 850×100, *T.I.S.S.*, viii, 102.
13   Castle Finlay, Rhigoul, Nairn, 105×45, *Arch. Scot.*, iv, 197.
14   Doune of Relugas, on Findhorn, Moray, 170×80.
15   Burghead, Moray.
16   Clunie Hill, Forres, ? Hibbert, *Arch. Scot.*, 160
17   Troupe Point, Banff, Hibbert, ibid.

---

[1] Arch. 110.   [2] *Proc.*, lxvii, 350; lxiii, 380.   [3] ibid., xlvii, 140.
[4] e.g. *Proc.*, lxvi, 72; lxi, 238; xliv, 215; lxvii, 350

ABERDEENSHIRE

18 Tap o' Noth, Huntly, F, 330×130.
19 Dunideer.

DEE TO TAY

20 Finella's Castle, Balbegno, small.
21 *Finavon*, on Esk near Aberlemno, FF, 475×110, *Trans. R. Soc. Literature*, 2, xi, 241; *P.S.A.S.*, lxix, 49.
22 Barra Hill, Alyth.
23 Dunsinane.
24 *Laws of Monifieth*, G–V, FF, 350×140, *P.S.A.S.*, iii, 441.
25 Dundee Law, F.

CENTRAL SCOTLAND

26 Machany, Muthil Station, Perths., F, 180×130, *P.S.A.S.*, lxxvii, 38.
27 Dun Mor, Sma' Glen, G, FF, 300×?.

WEST HIGHLANDS

28 The Bard's Castle, Bundalloch, W. Ross, 33×28.
29 Eilean Donan, Kintail, *T.I.S.S.*, viii, 109.
30 The Torr, R. Shiel.
31 Eilean nan Gobhar, Arisaig, 175×70, 75×25, *Arch. J.*, xxxvii, 1880, 239.
32 Ard Ghaunsgoik, Arisaig, 796×70, *Arch. J.*, 1880, 238.
33 Eilean Pt. na Muirach.
34 *Rahoy*, L. Teacuis, Morvern, FF, 40 diam., *P.S.A.S.*, lxxii, 23.
35 Lochan Gour, Ardgour, F, 250×30, *P.S.A.S.*, xliii, 43.
36 Onich, L. Leven, 41×30 rect., *P.S.A.S.*, xxiii, 374.
37 Dun Deardail, Glen Nevis, 180×110, *P.S.A.S.*, xxiii, 371.
38 *Dun Macuisneachan*, Connel, 750 long, F, *P.S.A.S.*, xi, 298; xii, pl. I.
39 Dun Beg, Dunstaffnage.
40 *Dun Troon*, L. Crinan, FF, 140×90, *P.S.A.S.*, xxxix, 275.
41 Dun Skeig, W. Loch Tarbert, Kintyre, 60×40, F, rect., *T.G.A.S.*, 1868, 31.
42 Carradale, Kintyre, F, 190×75.
43 Trudennish Pt., Islay, *P.S.A.S.*, lxix, 82.
44 Caisteal Aoidhe, Ardmarnock, Cowal, FF, 35×40.
45 Eilean Buidhe, Kyles of Bute, FF, 55 diam., *T.G.A.S.*, x, 65.
46 *Dunagoil*, Bute, FF, 300×75, *T.B.N.H.*, 1914–15, 1925.
47 An Knap, Sannox, Arran, ? 210×150, *P.S.A.S.*, lxii, 240.

SOUTH SHORES OF TAY ESTUARY

48 *Castle Law*, Abernethy, G, 180×90, *Proc.*, xxxiii, 18.
49 *Castle Law of Coltucher*, Forgandenny, G–V, 229×65 with outworks, 75 acres, *Proc.*, xxvii, 16.

SOUTH OF FORTH

51   Harelaw, Lammermuirs, R.C. *East Lothian*, No. 254.

SOUTH-EAST COASTS OF CLYDE FIRTH

52   Cumbrae, *T.G.A.S.*, 1862, 238.
53   Knock Hill, Largs, *Proc.*, lxxvii, 38.
54   Auldhill, Portencross, rect., 100 × 50, *Proc.*, lxxvii, 39.
55   Kildoun, Maybole, 150 × 100, *Proc.*, lxxvii, 39.
56   Dowhill, Girvan.
57   Kemp Law, Dundonald.

GALLOWAY

58   Dun o' May.
59   Trusty's Hillock, Anwoth.
60   Mote o' Mark, *Proc.*, xlviii, 125.
61   Castle Gower.

XII. ABBREVIATIONS

A.C.A.W.	.	*Archaeological Collections, Ayrshire and Wigtonshire.*
Arch.	.	*Archaeologia*, Society of Antiquaries of London.
Arch. J.	.	*Archaeological Journal*, Royal Archaeological Institute, London.
Arch. Scot.	.	*Archaeologia Scotica*, Society of Antiquaries of Scotland, Edinburgh.
Antiquity	.	*Antiquity*, Gloucester.
Ant. J.	.	*Antiquaries Journal*, Society of Antiquaries, London.
B.M.	.	British Museum.
B.N.C.	.	*Histories of the Berwickshire Naturalists' Club*, Berwick.
J.R.A.I.	.	*Journal of the Royal Anthropological Institute.*
Man	.	*Man*, Royal Anthropological Institute, London.
N.M.A.	.	National Museum of Antiquities, Edinburgh.
N.S.A.	.	*New Statistical Account of Scotland.*
O.S.A.	.	*(Old) Statistical Account of Scotland.*
P.C.B.I.	.	Childe, *Prehistoric Communities of the British Isles*, Edinburgh, 1940.
P.P.S.	.	*Proceedings of the Prehistoric Society*, Cambridge.
P.O.A.S.	.	*Proceedings of the Orkney Antiquarian Society*, Kirkwall.

P.S.E.A. . . . *Proceedings of the Prehistoric Society of East Anglia,* Norwich.

P.S.A.S. or Proc. *Proceedings of the Society of Antiquaries of Scotland,* Edinburgh.

R.C. . . . Royal Commission on Ancient and Historical Monuments (Scotland), *Inventory of Monuments in. . . .*

T.B.N.H. . . *Transactions of the Buteshire Natural History Society,* Rothesay.

T.D.G.A. . . . *Transactions of the Dumfries and Galloway Antiquarian and Natural History Society,* Dumfries.

T.G.A.S. . . . *Transactions of the Glasgow Archaeological Society* (new series).

T.G.S.I. . . . *Transactions of the Gaelic Society of Inverness.*

T.I.S.S. . . . *Transactions of the Inverness Scientific Society and Field Club.*

T.S.A.S. . . . *Transactions of the Stirling Archaeological Society.*

U.J.A. . . . *Ulster Archaeological Journal,* Belfast (third series).

Ure . . . *History of Rutherglen and Kilbride, Glasgow,* 1793.

INDEX

Abernethy (Castle Law), Perthshire, 14, 83, 91, 129, 135
Achnacree, Argyll, 98, 100
Adabrock, Lewis, 19, 71, 72, 131
adzes, 68
Agricola, Roman general, 15, 19, 129
agriculture, 24, 34, 43, 53, 70, 81, 91
amber, 59, 61, 72, 123, 133
Anderson, Joseph, 40, 92, 130
anvil-stones, 46
anvils, bronze, 68, 70
areas of settlements, 87–8
arrow-heads, 4, 7, 12, 24, 35, 44, 49, 70, 99, 119
Achnacree, Angus, 9, 58
authority of chiefs, 9, 60, 77, 95
axes:
  antler, 23
  stone, 4, 30, 46, 56, 99, 123, 132
  bronze, 12, 17, 46, 47, 56, 58, 68, 70, 71, 91, 130
  iron, 13, 81, 91, 94
Azilians, 3, 23

Balmashanner, Angus, 72, 73
Barger, E., 82
barley, 70, 79
battle-axes, 12, 64, 66, 77, 128
Beacharra pottery, 6, 40, 51, 98
beaches, raised, 3, 22, 23
beads:
  segmented fayence, 12, 128, 131
  bone, 33
  see also amber, gold, jet, necklaces
Beakers, 3, 7, 8, 16, 41 ff., 59, 79, 99, 101 ff.
beds, 28, 31, 32
Bersu, G., 14, 66
Blackwater Foot, Arran, 57, 60, 61, 120, 122
blood feud, 49
bloomeries, 12, 17, 80
bobbins, 84
Brackmont Mill, Fife, 63, 64, 66, 78, 102, 126, 128
brochs, 15, 17, 81, 89 ff., 128
brooches, 13, 19, 94, 129
bronze, 46, 55, 68, 70

burial:
  collective, 3, 37, 41, 42
  double, 33, 43, 120
  individual, 7, 16, 41, 42, 44, 49
  extended, 10, 60, 119
  see also cremation
buttons, 57

Calder, C. S. T., 18
Callander, J. G., 9, 43, 128, 132
Camster, Caithness, 42, 100
carpentry, 56, 70
castles, 89 ff.
cattle (bovids), 24, 26, 34, 52, 83
cauldrons, 12, 68, 74, 85
Celts, 79, 95
cemeteries, 9, 10, 34, 38, 52, 63 ff., 134
chambered cairns, 3, 7, 18, 34–9, 41–2, 55, 97 ff., 103
chariots, 93
chiefs, 49, 60, 76, 89, 95
chronology:
  relative, 1, 14, 16, 42, 50, 63, 99, 103, 123, 130, 131, 133
  absolute, 14, 18, 128–32
circles, see Recumbent, and Stone
Cinerary Urns, 10, 11, 63 ff., 124 f., 130, 134
clans, 33, 38, 41, 42, 44, 48, 62, 64, 73
Clark, J. G. D., 9
classes, division of society into, 95
Clava cairns, 5, 40, 50, 97, 104
Collessie, Fife, 49, 57, 121
combs, weaving, 84
commodity production, 46, 56, 60, 73, 75, 84
communism, primitive, 33, 38, 62, 75, 94
co-operation, social, 32, 37
craftsmen's tools, 68, 70, 91
Craw, J. H., 9, 59
crannogs, 15, 85
cremation, 10, 16, 18, 40, 50, 61, 63, 76, 103, 105, 120, 134
crucibles, 87, 91, 94
cups, imported bronze, 19, 71, 131
cupboards, 28
Curle, A. O., 17, 52, 54, 56, 72, 80, 86
Curle, James, 129
Curwen, E. C., 82

LIST OF PLATES

1

2

3

I

2

1

2

IV

1

2

1

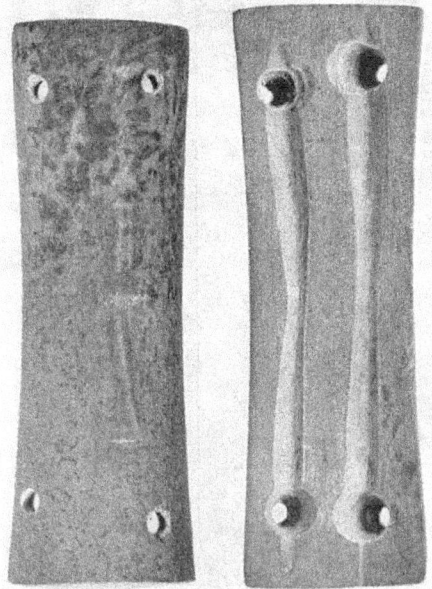

2

3

4

1

2

3

4

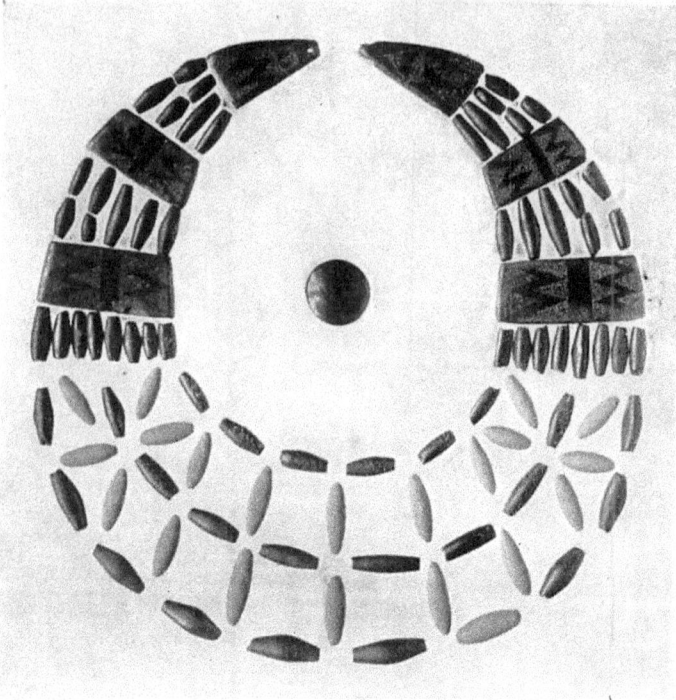

I

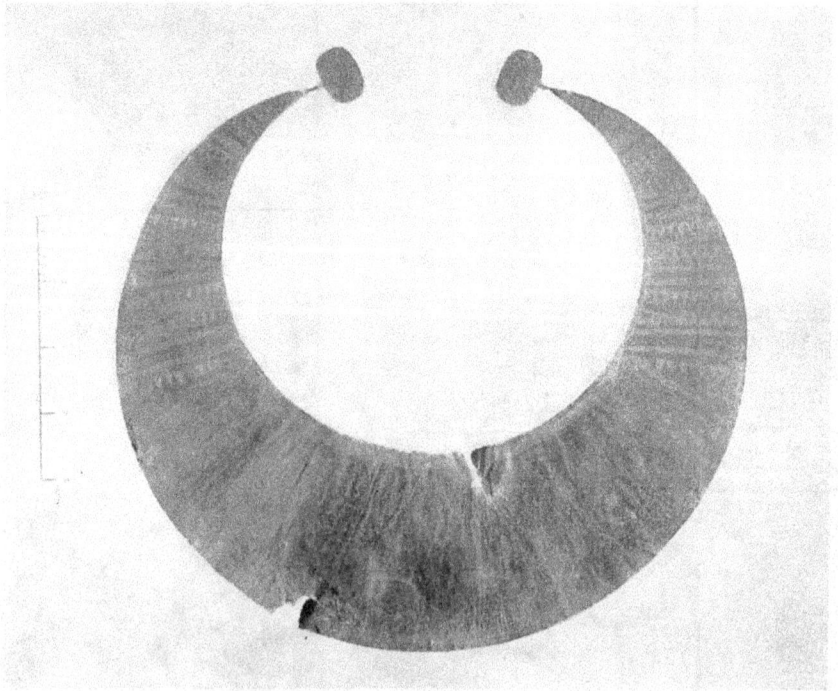

2

1

2

X

I

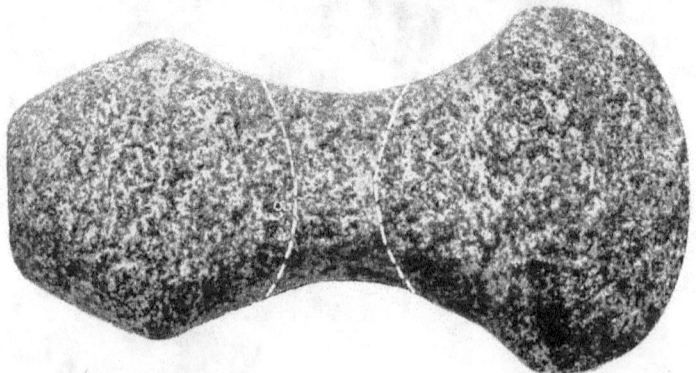

3

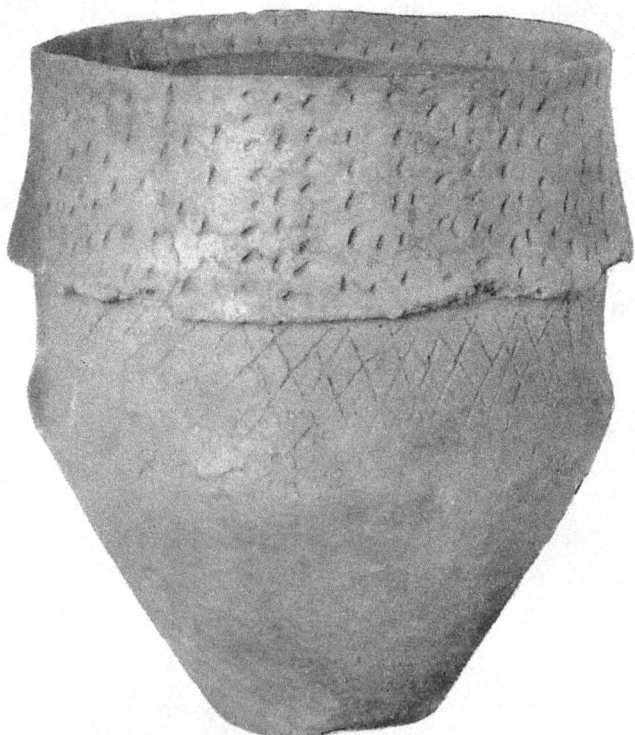
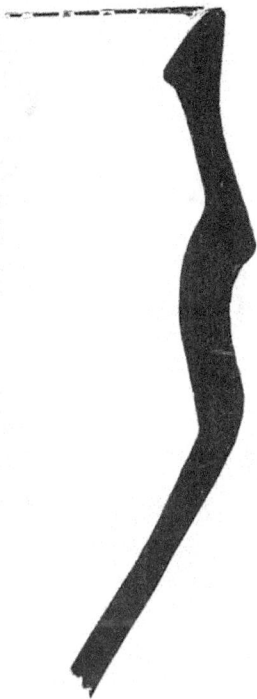

1

2

3

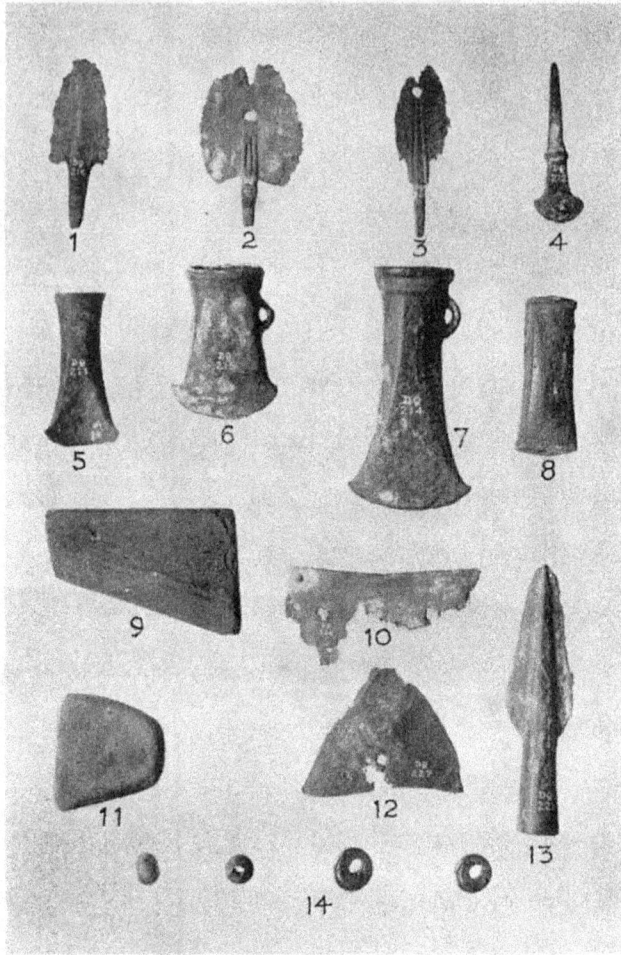

1

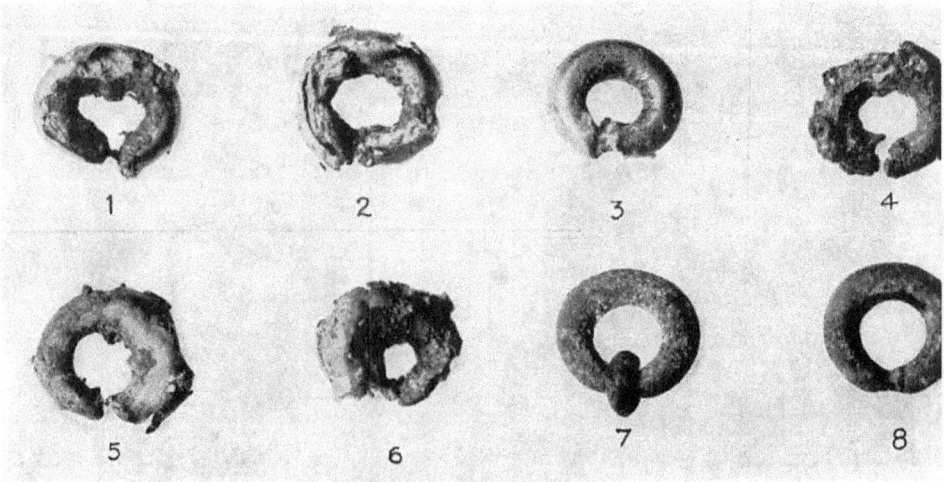

2

1

2

I

2

1

2

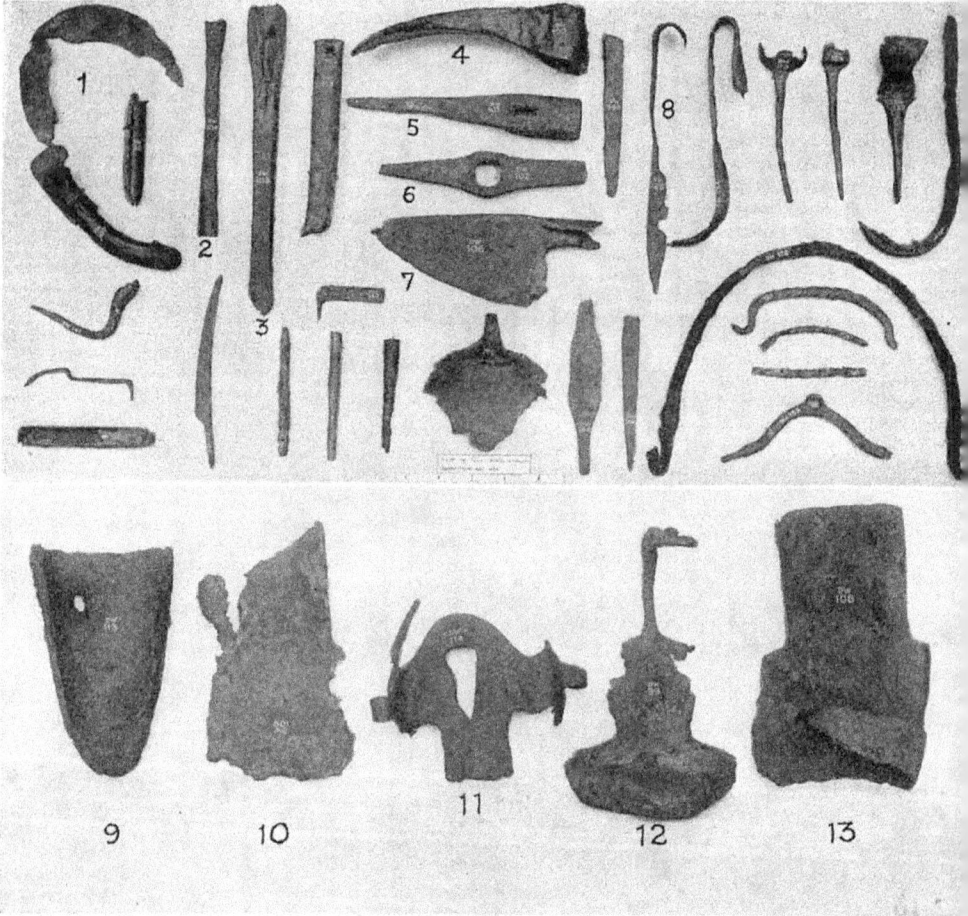

For Product Safety Concerns and Information please contact our EU
representative GPSR@taylorandfrancis.com
Taylor & Francis Verlag GmbH, Kaufingerstraße 24, 80331 München, Germany

www.ingramcontent.com/pod-product-compliance
Lightning Source LLC
Chambersburg PA
CBHW050519280326
41932CB00014B/2376

9 781032 070346